Claude McNeal's Miracle in Springs Valley

The Amazing Story of Two Grand Hotels

Photo Design by MaryLou Szczesiul

Illustrated by Marilyn Longmire

Miracle in Springs Valley
ISBN: 978-0-615-37647-9

Copyright 2010 by Claude McNeal
All Rights Reserved

Illustrations Copyright 2010 by Marilyn Longmire
All Rights Reserved

Sections Reprinted by Permission

1st Edition 2010
2nd Edition 2016
3rd Edition 2021

CMcN Books
P.O. Box 441130
Zip 46244
tel: 317-916-0568

Introduction

When I was invited in the 1980s to bring my theatrical company from New York City to the French Lick Springs Hotel in Indiana to do three of my shows in repertory there, it was my first trip to the Midwest. As I found time to get out and about I fell in love with the rolling hills, the down-to-earth-ness of the people, and started learning the incredible history of two grand hotels that evolved over many years right here in what is called 'Springs Valley.' At that time West Baden Springs Hotel was not in operation. So I wrote *The Making of A Grand Hotel* about French Lick Springs. Years later when the Cook family decided to undertake the miraculous re-doing of both grand hotels, I was inspired to write the whole story --complete with the happy ending. It is an amazing story, and is very much a part of the American story itself.

-Claude McNeal

Dedicated to my wife Janet, who grew up in Orange County.

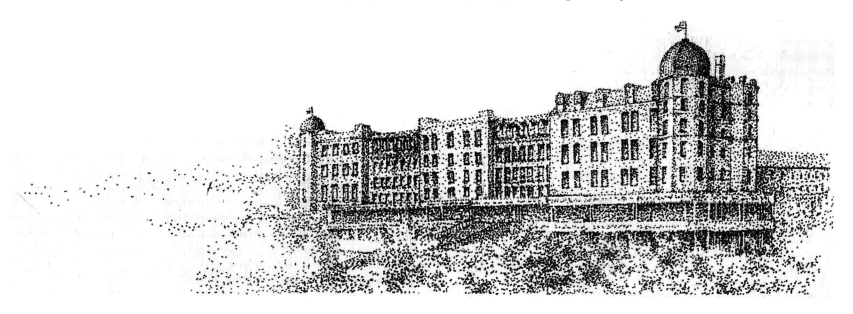

Part One

The Early Days of Springs Valley

IN THE BEGINNING...

We all wonder what it must have been like --years and years ago...
We know that in ancient times millions of years ago a great sea caused, with its ebb and flow, those rolling hills here in what we now call Indiana. We know that the receding sea left a mineral and biological richness to the new land, which brought us a myriad of animal and plant life. Over the many years of development, these new vibrant forms of life evolved, with grandeur and magnificence. In its midst was a rich plant valley with salt wells that seeped to the surface, and over the years played host to thousands of plant and animal life forms, eventually humans. Shortly after the turn of the 20th Century, it also housed two of the grandest of hotels, now with a bountiful heritage.

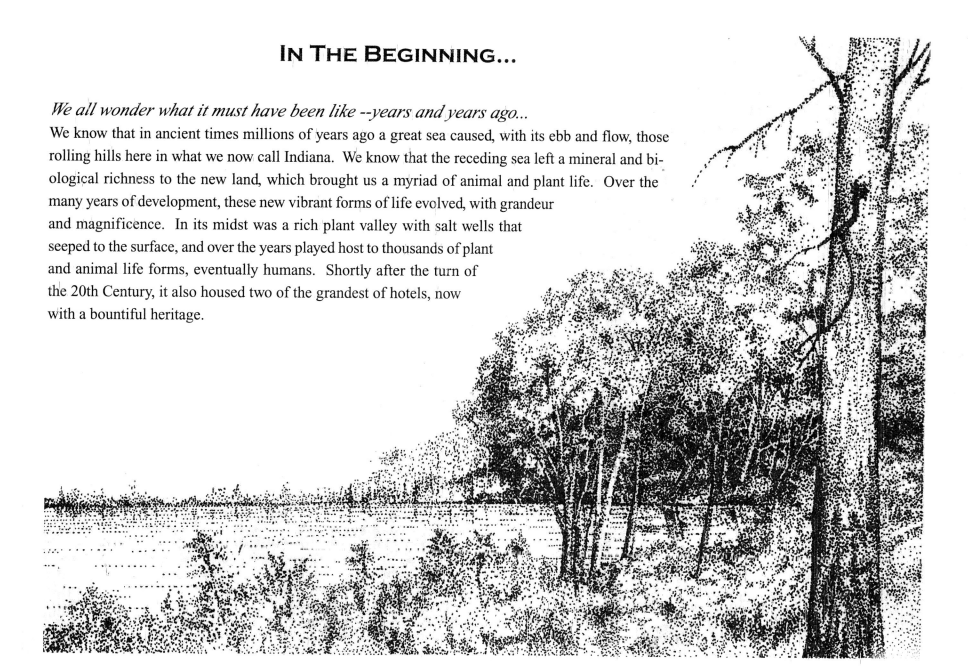

For millions of years, the American buffalo (bison), and other noble beasts, roamed these changing lands. The buffalo formed what we call today "buffalo traces" –paths—that took them for hundreds of miles on a nomadic journey, many miles a day, much as the birds over head fly place to place, season to season. The birds take the shortest, most direct journey. And, mysteriously, so did the buffalo.

It is predicted that not so long ago 80,000,000 buffalo roamed these lands as their own. They had their own system of work and play – they would forage for food from the enormous amount of vegetation along the way, and they would form large mud holes by lounging in the swampy areas –to cool off! One of the great buffalo traces for hundreds of years was between the first established town in Indiana, Vincennes on the Wabash, and 'the falls' (now Louisville) on the Ohio River. Halfway in between, the herds stopped to pause and be refreshed with a special luxury --the salt that rose up from the underground springs, then caked on stones. This half-way 'resort' along the buffalo trace would host 500 buffalo at a time, who stopped to lick the salted rocks.

Using the buffalo trails, and virtually living off them for food and clothing, came the Indians, the various tribes that inhabited the land over thousands of years; then a few hundred years ago, it was known as the Indiana Territory.

As we know, the Indians preceded the White man here by many years and survived on the abundance of animal life, and the fertile soil.

They emerged from, or were followed by, the mysterious Mound Builders, as we call them today, who built mounds which to this day have no logical explanation for their existence. One, just ten miles from where the hotels stand today, is three feet high, 1300 feet long, and has divulged many artifacts from this early race of humans. At one time these mounds were likely much larger. (Sketched here is one of the few remarkable pieces of sculpture that has been found --a contemplative 'thinker' looking into the future.)

So, long before the traders and trappers arrived on the scene in the 18th Century, there were those ancient tribes now called the Mississippian culture, whose works to this day are a marvel of sophistication and creative energy. How closely they are allied to the Indian tribes that followed is hard to tell, but it is fitting that virtually all previous inhabitants of this Southern Indiana area, man and beast, have found solace and enchantment in the valley of French Lick and West Baden—now commonly referred to as Springs Valley.

We know that the French arrived here in the later 1700s. They came up from the New Orleans area on their way to Canada, using traces and rivers. These early French travelers were trappers and tradesmen, and they set up many outposts along the Wabash River. A sturdy lot, many recently out of European prisons, they became in a way the first 'cowboys' in what was then the wild West. Some drifted inland from the rivers, established friendly relations with the Northern Indians. Unfortunately, the great diversity of tribes caused many conflicts. The resultant French and Indian War became the major factor in changing the tide in favor of the English, then other incoming groups, such as the Germans. But the French had left their mark, with their great Daniel Boone-style coonskin hats, bear grease, and furs of all kinds – many traded to the Indians.

A New Country

By 1779 there was an attempt to clear the land of Indians. Because most of the French had already moved farther West, the Indians were becoming more predominate. A general of the U.S. Army took a trip up the buffalo trace from the Ohio to Vincennes. His name was George Rogers Clark, and when he stopped off at the now famous resting place with the salt rocks, he and his officers dubbed it "French Lick."

Clark's excursion ran into some trouble as it reached French Lick. Dissention hit the ranks and there was an insubordination trial of one of his officers. But after the problem got "settled," apparently the feasting began. It is reported that "the hunting was magnificent" because prey came from miles to the 'salt lick' to be met by fire from the muskets of Clark's soldiers. It was days before the soldiers marched on.

INDIANA TERRITORY

There were problems with that new expanding section of America, the Indiana Territory: trading posts, once French, were taken over by the British, there were constant battles between the tribes from the Southern territory and the Northern Iroquois Indians armed with muskets from the Dutch in New York. Ongoing raids of the villages by both the Indians and the Whites were frequent.

By 1800 the population of the Indiana Territory was about 6,500 Whites and 25,000 Indians whose leaders signed an Ordinance in 1787 that promised that their lands and property "shall never be taken away from us without our consent." Many treaties, signed in 1804 and 1805 by chiefs of the various tribes, were causes of great dissention within the tribes, as they felt that their chiefs had betrayed them. Therefore many Indians went on the warpath, and the White settlers were ordered by the US government to build blockhouses for their own protection. US Rangers were sent to patrol these areas and one of the largest blockhouses (forts) was built on the grounds that the French Lick Springs Hotel presently stands on.

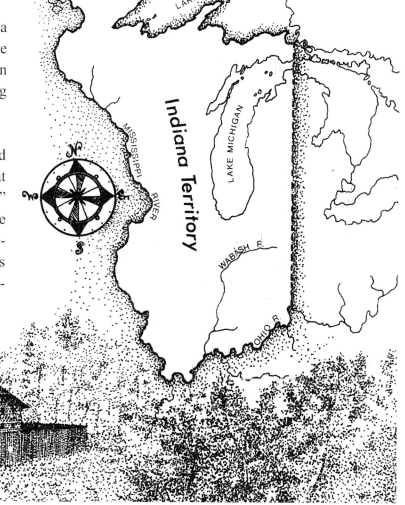

All across the country sad tales of battles between the White settlers and the already settled Indians were heard. Many forts were set up, and for a number of years raiding parties of one group against the other were every day events. Many were lost on both sides, often by hideous scalping by the Red Man or terrible maiming by the White Man. It is early America's saddest legacy. It is perhaps ironic that this most tragic beginning of America became the very symbol of good and evil in stories, plays, eventually Hollywood movies, and even, children at play: Cowboys vs. Indians.

From the 1600s to the 1800s in the Indiana Territory, it is mainly a story of the Miami tribes securing the land, meeting and trading with the White traders, fighting off hostile tribes from surrounding areas, and defending themselves against the warring Iroquois and many Nomadic tribes, principally of Algonquian stock.

The Miamis formed a liaison with French Jesuits, who had come from France to organize a new world where religion, economics, and politics would coincide to uplift the 'savage Indians,' and honor civilization as it was practiced in France by King Louis XIV. By the time the Jesuits founded the settlement of St. Louis, they had made the disturbing discovery that the Indian tribes had virtually been eliminated. Soon, the Jesuits departed the beautiful wilderness of the Indiana Territory. One of those places was French Lick.

In the early 1800s at the blockhouse at French Lick, the soldiers often prepared for attacks. One can imagine looking out from the fort from one direction and seeing the animals gather up to lick the salt from the stones becoming easy musket prey, and in another direction the area farmers planting "Indian corn" and other vegetables. An 'eye witness' reporting on a 'personal observation' in 1812, gives a flavor of the times:

The Indians were offended at one William Charles, a married man, and were determined on his death. To accomplish the deed they laid around in the dense forest and from their hiding places in the hills they saw Charles ploughing corn near the French Lick Fort. On the night following, they hid behind a stump of a large tree that had been chopped down for timber in building the fort. Charles came in the morning and all day long followed the plow across the field uninterrupted. Late that evening, just as the sun was setting, the treacherous Indians fired the fatal shot and Charles fell dead in the furrow.

The Indians made a rush for his scalp, but the sound of the gun alarmed the soldiers of the fort, and they made a dash for the corn field. The Indians fled, never more to return. Their revenge was accomplished and they hastened to join the members of their tribe in the Land of the Setting Sun.

William Charles is buried where the hotel now stands, and some think his ghost still haunts the area.

A New Beginning

Nearly every state has an exciting story of its birth. Indiana, still part of a territory at the turn of the 19th Century, was going through the struggle to become a state, when it, in 1815, finally attained the necessary 60,000 population set up as a minimum for statehood by the Northwest Ordinance. On December 11, 1816, the necessary appeal to the US Congress was approved, and the delegates put together a constitution. The Congress accepted Indiana as the 19th State!

The principal problem facing the new state was, simply, land travel. Still one of the few roads in Southern Indiana was the one from the Falls at the Ohio that ran west past French Lick, to Vincennes at the Wabash, along the old buffalo trace. Soon towns were growing along it with new settlers emigrating mainly from Virginia and the Carolinas. By 1820, Indiana had a growing population of new arrivals, perhaps 65,000, excluding Nomadic Indians. Eager to compete in the growing world of commerce, and settle into its own identity, Indiana built more roads, improved public necessities in its growing towns, and built public buildings. And by the time a thought of a hotel in the salt valley was considered in the late 1830s, Indiana had become a booming pioneer state in a growing nation.

Coming of Age

It is hard for us to realize today how difficult it was to preserve food in the not-so-long-ago time before refrigeration. By the early 1800s, smoking food, drying it, or salting it, were the primary methods of food preservation. In the northern states winter ice was packed underground in sawdust heaps to be kept for summer. So it must have been exciting for the first settlers and cavalry at the French Lick Fort, to be able to simply go to the surrounding rocks, scrape off the salt, and use it as a food preservative. As a matter of fact, by 1818 it is reported by a traveler from Jeffersonville to Vincennes, that there were many recently erected 'homes in the area of the Lick', and that many had signs up that "board and lodging could be had within." Many sported salt-preserved meat. Luxury had come. So important was salt, suddenly, to the area, that the newly formed state government decreed an enabling act that called for limited leasing of French Lick land in order to protect the new saline reserve.

"To manufacture salt"

The earliest method was simply to boil the water until only the salt remained. Kettles over an open fire were used for the boiling. But the method proved too un-productive for commercial use, because there was not a high enough quantity of salt in the water.

In 1830, the state went to great lengths to attempt to get a productive amount of salt. With new machinery, they bored down to a depth of 200 feet. But this attempt, too, did not produce enough salt, and by 1832, the state and congress were ready to 'lease or sell' the land. At the same time, there was much talk and concern around Indiana about "internal improvements," principally more new roads. Ironically one way the state hoped to gain revenue was by selling off land at French Lick. A proposal for a major wider road that would also go beyond the buffalo trace from the Ohio to Vincennes was put forward, considered, and eventually implemented. The area became more accessible to newcomers.

In 1833 and 1834, a Thomas C. Bowles purchased a parcel of land in French Lick, most likely because of its new accessibility, and shortly afterward assigned this land to his son, Dr. William A. Bowles.

THE DREAM

The fabulous story of what was to become the first grand hotel in the mid-West -- French Lick Springs Hotel – begins in the 1830s in the mind of young Dr. Bowles. William A. Bowles was born in 1799 in Maryland. His parents recently had come from England to Frederick County, Maryland, then moved to Orange County, Indiana, settling in Paoli –nine short miles from French Lick.

A contemporary described Bowles as:

very handsome and physically perfect, six feet two inches in height and two hundred pounds. His personality was very remarkable. He had a soft and musical but powerful voice. He always had a pleasant smile and sincere manner. He possessed great intelligence and was respected throughout the community for his wisdom and great stock of general knowledge. A man with such a magnetic personality was naturally an influential person in his community.

Little is known of Bowles' education, but by 1831 he was a practicing physician, surgeon, and clergyman.

William Bowles did not at first establish himself as a hotel builder. Rather he became the most famous doctor in Southern Indiana in a very short time. Paoli had a population of 400 in those early years. As a surgeon, Bowles took on the most difficult cases, and was constantly called upon to minister to the desperately ill. He also established himself as a concerned citizen for social causes in the area, and developed a strong, ardent following. But his major interest was soon to turn to business, then to politics, and then to the military. It is without a question that this fascinating, and eventually controversial man, was to become the founder, if only in his wild hopes at the time, of a new way of relaxation and enjoyment in the Valley of Salt Springs.

One of the most famous phrases in American 19th Century history is Horace Greeley's "Go West, young man, go West!" At that time the vast majority of the American people lived on the east coast. When Indiana gained statehood, it was considered a western state.

A map of the time would show many of the original thirteen colonies with large extensions to the West. It seemed that the original states would someday extend across the country.

The great areas of land that had earlier been claimed by the various European countries were broken up over the next 100 years into the states as we know them today: the Louisiana Purchase, the Indiana Territory, the Oregon Territory, California, Texas, etc., which were also the sites of the battles of extension.

While great struggles, and general hard times were faced by those early pioneers, Greeley's dictum became the reality: America moved West. New trails and roads brought many past the already established way stations, such as the one Dr. Bowles had established in 'the valley of the salt wells.'

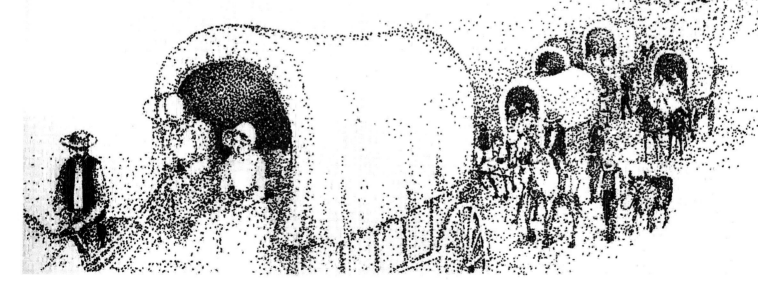

Horace Greeley
1811-1872

That First Hotel

We have only a few reports about the first hotel, called 'French Lick House,' but they are interesting because of their candor. A contemporary, A.J. Rhodes recalled:

I can not tell of what order of architecture it was, but as I remember to its peculiar style, I conclude it was his [Bowles'] own conception of a builidng of that kind, and that it was original. I think it was perhaps 80 to 100 feet long, rather narrow and three stories high. The house was a frame with a strange appearance. The rafters were nearby perpendicular. A two-story structure extended south perhaps some forty feet.

Rhodes doesn't give a date for when he saw the hotel, and there is no exact date to be found. Some theories place the constructing of the hotel as early as 1836, but most place the date in the mid 1840s. The first direct reference to its existence is in an 1845 July 4th celebration "at Dr. Bowles' new building in French Lick."

Certainly, by then, the new 'highway' from the Ohio to the Wabash was used as a stopping off place, and French Lick was ideally located. And the enterprising Dr. Bowles, whose fortune and fame were growing, must have lured the patrons to his hotel.

The Mexican War

Quickly shifting political factors in 1845-1846 drew the country into the Mexican War. After James K. Polk was elected president, he immediately set about annexation proceedings for both Oregon and Texas. These moves, in time, caused the beginning of that brief, but ferociously fought war, declared on May 13, 1846 against Mexico. Bowles, who besides starting a new hotel had been elected to the state legislature, decided to join the army. So he leased his new hotel to a Dr. John A. Lane, and used his political connections to become a commissioned officer for the Indiana contingent. Soon they proudly marched to Texas to fight the Mexicans.

What actually happened to Bowles in that war is reported diversely, but it is known that an American force of 5,000 was confronted by 20,000 Mexican soldiers. Bowles, a commissioned colonel, was in charge of 360 men from the Indiana brigade who were confronted with a surprise attack by 7,000 Mexican soldiers. As the story goes, Bowles, not knowing that other officers of the Indiana contingency wanted to stand and fight, ordered his men to retreat. In their haste, some soldiers trampled those behind them. The whole incident became a rout for Bowles and his men. But after the troops scattered, Bowles, with a few remainders, joined a Mississippi contingent –and stayed to see the American victory that ended the 'Mexican' War.

The Enterprise of 'Doctor' John Lane

Meanwhile, John A. Lane, who peddled patent medicines, and was occasionally listed as a physician, set out to establish the hotel in his own image. While Bowles was gone, Lane made 'improvements on the inn,' and discovered the route to profit would be in promoting the salt springs. But when Bowles returned to Indiana in 1854 he suddenly took back his lease on the hotel and set up shop again.

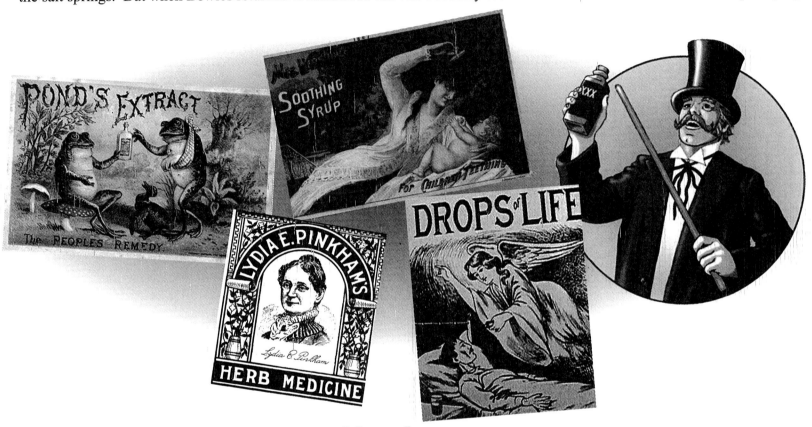

Mile Lick

However, unknown to Bowles at the time, Lane had purchased land a mile north of the French Lick Hotel. It was called 'Mile Lick,' and it was where Lane went to set up a competitive 'inn' of his own. Lane began an aggressive competition from his 'new' resort, and soon changed the name from 'Mile Lick' to "West Baden," after the European resort famous for its renowned mineral springs. Soon the popularity of the two 'resorts' in the valley soared, mainly because of the one ingredient: salt flavored water from the many springs in the magical valley.

ANCIENT HEALTH RESORTS

Salt springs were far from a new phenomenon in 19th Century America. In Greek mythology, early mineral health resorts are referred to as having 'miraculous healing powers.' In Hesiod's history of Greece he refers to a group of mineral water enthusiasts who were called the cult of Asclepius who, in the 5th Century BC, oversaw mineral water health 'resorts' in the Grecian Empire. (Asclepius, the Greek god of healing, born of Apollo and mortal maiden Corinis, carried a staff with a serpent twisting around it that is now the universal symbol for medicine.) They created popular retreats at Epidaurus, Cos, Corinth, and other locations. Soon the Romans adopted the practice of using cleansing, healing mineral water for health purposes, also. At the height of the Roman Empire, the city had thirteen aqueducts, 1352 public fountains, 962 public baths, and a system for public bathing to improve health: first step into a warm bath (tepidarium), then to a hot bath (caldarium), then into a sweat room. Then there would be a cold water plunge (frigidarium) to purge the body of impurities.

It is recorded that the Mayans of the Yucatan Peninsula also used thermal springs therapeutically as far back as the 4th Century BC. Also there are various mentions in the Christian Bible of miraculous cures with water. Perhaps the most remarkable example of the enduring lure of mineral waters is that Baden, a famous spa in Switzerland, has been in continuous operation for over 2,000 years –since 61 BC.

Certainly, over the centuries the many locations that sported mineral springs, became the 'resort' of choice for many in centuries to come.

There came a time in America when mineral water was promoted as something that would cure the body's ills. It was a new curative liquid –that also could 'cleanse the body, enhance the soul, and soothe the mind.' It was the miracle that made possible a better life!

WHAT'S IN MINERAL WATER

Mineral water begins as natural water flowing underground, but its special nature is that, in its travels, it takes on a quantity of salts and gases from the rocks and soil over which it flows, thus altering it into 'mineral' water, seeping into reachable wells.

While mineral waters are usually clear, it also can be whitish because of suspended calcium carbonate, or free sulfur. It can be bluish because of suspended clay or slate, or reddish because of a suspension of red iron oxide.

On the downside, a bitter taste in some mineral waters is due to magnesium sulphate, or sodium sulphate; mineral water with a salty taste is due to the presence of sodium chloride.

Mineral waters containing hydrogen sulphide can have a penetrating odor akin to rotten eggs, which was the case in some of the springs in the French Lick Valley in the early days. But over time, ways were found to lessen the odor and improve the taste, and mineral waters from Springs Valley in Indiana would eventually be sold across the country. So the mineral water springs in 'Springs Valley' gave the area its nickname and the word of its curative powers spread to a growing population.

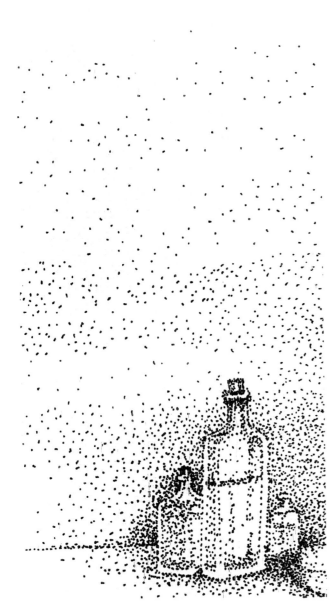

Travel

In the early days, transportation was always a distinct challenge. Rivers and canals were common means of travel, but dirt roads, often rutted or made impassible by relentless rains and mud, predominated in remote areas such as Springs Valley. A lot of progress would be needed before two extraordinary grand hotels would evolve into two of the greatest vacation escapes in America. But the progress was soon to begin.

MacAdam

Imagine so exciting a time as when new 'MacAdamized' highways (early asphalt) made roads solid for travel on the old buffalo traces! MacAdam was a new way of constructing roads where layers of soil and compressed gravel were covered with a sand, gravel and tar mix that would 'waterproof' the under layers, allowing for drainage, that would keep the road 'solid.' 'MacAdam' was invented by Scottish engineer John London McAdam in the early 19th Century, and made its way to Southern Indiana a half century later. Now over-land stage coaches could more easily travel to French Lick. This enhanced the quality and quantity of travel so much that both John Lane and William Bowles, who by now were laying out plans 'to improve the life' of all the people in the entire area, got the biggest boost of patronage ever at their hotels.

WEST BADEN INN

Meanwhile in West Baden, Lane borrowed $1,800 to capitalize a sawmill, from which he was able to cut lumber for new construction on his hotel. And he added a bridge across French Lick Creek. With its own mineral water springs, his new 'hotel,' 'West Baden Inn,' became as popular as Mr. Bowles' hotel a mile down the road. And the competition became fierce.

BOWLES' CIVIL WAR

Not to be outdone, William Bowles added a grist mill, store house, steam mill, drug house, and most importantly, a facility to bottle mineral water. But his politics took him toward the preservation of slavery, just at a time when the whole notion of owning slaves was becoming suspect across much of the nation. Because Bowles and his wife deeply believed in the institution of slave ownership, she and Bowles put together "The Knights of the Golden Circle," a pro-slavery group which dangerously included people in the 'Northern' state of Indiana. Bowles went from town to town attempting to convince people of his philosophical leanings, but when the Civil War began, the tide turned and people who were losing sons and husbands to the South had a hard time tolerating someone on their side espousing the views of the enemy. Bowles was arrested and tried for treason, convicted and imprisoned. But shortly before he was to be hanged, in a dramatic moment, President Lincoln commuted his sentence to life imprisonment.

The turmoil caused by the war was immense. It was America's bloodiest war in history. Kinship and loyalty that only a few short years earlier was taken for granted came under suspicion. Brother did fight brother. The blue and the grey became symbols of the meaning of life itself, in America. Indiana was at the center of much of the 'turmoil,' because the South and the North divided at the Indiana/Kentucky border. By the end of the war, just after Lincoln's assassination in a war-weary nation, there was a presidential pardon ordered by President Andrew Johnson, and Bowles was set free. But he came back to his house in Indiana a broken man. No longer did he take part in political activities; he remained subdued, and a changed man. He was never able to live down his public disgrace, and on top of this Bowles also had to take up defending himself against his new wife who was now suing him for divorce. As Shakespeare wrote, "After the thunder, cometh the rain."

The Knights of the Golden Circle
(An organization in the north, led by Bowles that favored slavery. The leading members were brought to trial for treason and sentenced to be hanged.)

Pluto's Well

In 1869, a Dr. D.J. Rogers came to French Lick to analyze the contents of the mineral waters, and gave the water high praise. He also dubbed it Pluto's Well. The name stuck. Dr. Bowles soon advertised the powers on the 'curative waters' from his French Lick Springs thusly:

Dysepia in all its varieties, Chronic Dysentary and Diarrhae (sic) Loss of Appetite, Jaundice affections of the Liver, Splean (sic) and Kidneys, Murcurial diseases in all varieties, Diseases of the Skin, and ulcers of the most formidable character are annually relieved and cured here.

Then, lo and behold, on the grounds of French Lick Springs Hotel newly discovered mineral water Springs caused a three year surge of growth for the hotel. But Bowles' health began to decline, and he leased his hotel to a Dr. Samuel Ryan, who, in his tenure, improved the buildings, and the surrounding area of the hotel, giving it its first touches of grandeur.

More Troubles

Bowles' three marriages had many difficulties. But his second brief marriage was the most difficult. Eliza (later killed in a riverboat accident), tried to gain the property in one of the most famous divorce cases in Southern Indiana history. Bowles –after defeat in the Orange County Circuit Court –appealed to the Indiana Supreme Court. There he was defeated on grounds of "improper conduct" and ordered to pay a substantial alimony. Upon his failure to pay, the money was taken from his estate, and Bowles went into another personal decline, including new health problems.

Meanwhile, the hotel continued taking on a life of its own under new management. Additions were undertaken on the main structure, and a general upgrading of the property was accomplished as more Americans, now in a Reconstruction boom a decade after the war, were hearing about it and visiting in increasing numbers.

Bowles died in 1873 in the midst of yet another controversy – the true ownership of the hotel property. He left no will and his second and third wives were to individually battle over the property. It was in the early 1880s when the third Mrs. Bowles, Julia, won the majority of the property. She promptly sold it to Hirem W. Wells and James M. Andrews who became the first of a succession of owners taking the hotel up to the turn of the century when stability in ownership would once more return.

After Bowles' death, Lane continued to run his West-Baden hotel another decade then sold it a few months before his death in 1883. The new owners of both hotels continued improvements, but an era had come to an end with both Bowles and Lane gone from the scene.

Time marched on.

INVENTIONS

In the larger world beyond Springs Valley, America was going through an enormous technological change that would greatly effect the way people lived day-to-day. It was the beginning of an era of new inventions that improved human travel, communication, entertainment, food preservation, and more. It all took place in a brief 30-year period beginning in the 1870s and became an explosion of more major inventions than in all the rest of human history, before or since. These included: the electric light, the telephone, the phonograph, the motion picture, the radio, the automobile, the airplane, refrigeration, the process of pasteurizing food, etc. And these inventions, many by Thomas A. Edison, were soon to reach French Lick and West Baden.

While these inventions would greatly add to the future of the Valley, an earlier invention was to make the first big difference.

The Railway

That earlier invention was the locomotive, pulling a line of freight or passenger cars on a track of parallel iron or steel rails placed on a permanent 'roadway.' It was called the Railway. While there are various early versions of horse-pulled trains, it was in 1820 that the first steam powered locomotive was invented, and soon throughout America and Europe, there was a great surge of laying railroad lines by armies of railroad men who moved millions of tons of earth, built thousands of bridges, and laid miles and miles of 'track.' In the second half of the 19th Century, railways started to criss-cross the nation and brought a new kind of commerce to the country. The Transcontinental Railway, completed in 1869 with the last spike driven in at Promontory Utah, became the railroad's symbol of great achievement. In June of 1888 the French Lick Springs Hotel management signed a contract with the Louisville, New Albany and Chicago Railroad, granting them a right of way to the hotel grounds. Within a year track was laid into French Lick connecting the rail line to the rest of the nation. It was the Monon Railway. Eventually, people could reach French Lick and West Baden from virtually anywhere in America. And there was a great building surge, first at the French Lick Springs Hotel.

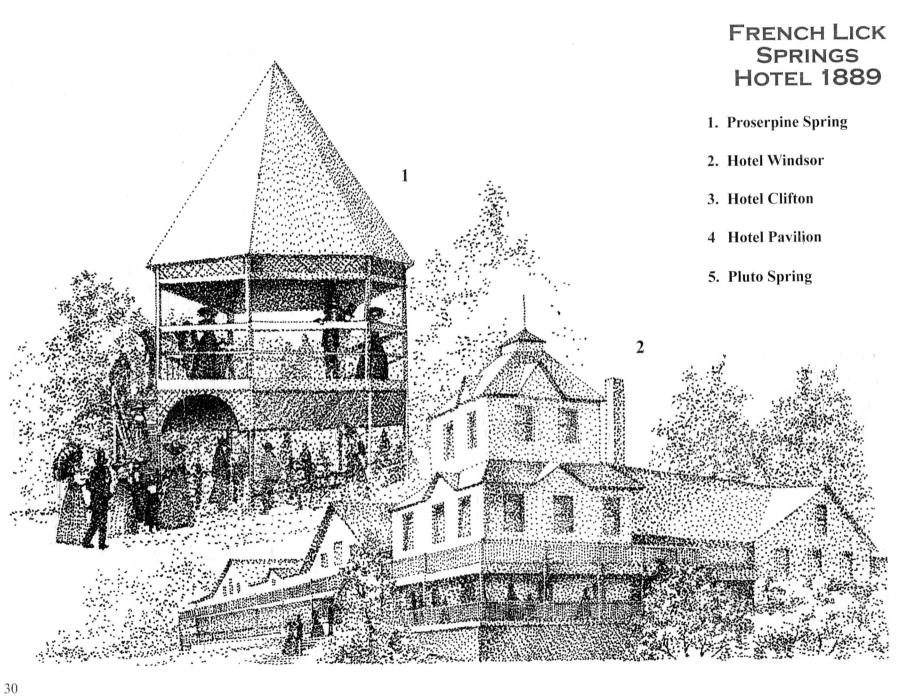

YEAR - ROUND

In the 1880s, even while both hotels were upgrading their buildings and becoming more successful, they were, surprisingly, operating only during summer months. Then, new heating and water systems were added to both hotels, and with the new railway service to both hotels, they were able to start operating year-round. Now the valley became one of the prized places to visit, year-round, in the nation. A new day was dawning.

The earliest known photo of the West Baden Springs Hotel (undated).

The earliest known photograph of the French Lick Springs Hotel (undated).

LEE WILEY SINCLAIR

The most important event in the history of the West Baden Hotel is when, in the late 1880s, a highly successful banker and businessman, Lee Wiley Sinclair, of nearby Salem Indiana, set his mind on purchasing the hotel.

Born in 1836 in Cloverdale Indiana, the young Sinclair's family moved to Greencastle Indiana, where he grew up working in his father's warehouse. He married Eliza Bredit, and moved to Salem, where he soon showed his business acumen by building a large woolen mill. After a stint in the Civil War, Sinclair returned to his business enterprises. He expanded his holdings to include a dry goods department store in Salem, and a textile mill in Chicago, and soon became one of the wealthiest men in Indiana.

He eventually won a seat in the Indiana House of Representatives in 1887-1889. It was at this time that Sinclair saw that there was a great future for a hotel with a railroad connection to the country at large. He obviously saw the future potential of a year round heated hotel. After aggressively negotiating over an extended period of time with the various owners, in 1888 Mr. Sinclair was able to become an owner himself in the growing enterprise of West Baden Springs Hotel. Springs Valley soon became filled with activity.

The Paoli Republican declared in July 1888, "The hotels at both places have never had such a run. Both are going to build large additions. A building boom has struck this place. The owners are expecting their biggest season yet."

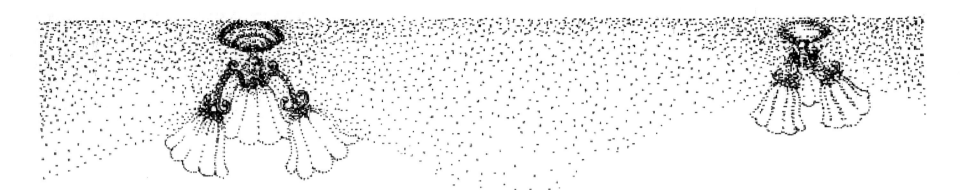

Additions

Meanwhile at the French Lick Springs Hotel, more was added: new furniture nearly everywhere, a new pavilion, and a large whiteframe building to be used for dining and entertainment was constructed. Also added were a beautiful brand new dining room, an engine room, water works (that eventually supplied water for the whole town), an ice house, and even a cold storage room. In 1890 the entire grounds were wired for electricity, which was also added to every single room, making it one of the first hotels in the country to be so equipped. Room rates rose to $2.00 - $3.50 a day, depending upon location. Dr. Ryan, now getting along in years, was made house physician, and many more personnel were added, including a house photographer. It was just a few years after Edison invented the electric light in 1879 that "incandescent bells" were placed throughout the hotel. Even a permanent band was hired. Often, 1,000 guests a night were at French Lick Springs – "the world's first modernized Grand Hotel," they called themselves.

In the 1890s as a new owner of the West Baden Springs Hotel, Lee Wiley Sinclair began plans for buying out his partners and adding his own structures that eventually molded the West Baden Hotel in a new image. He added a swimming pool, gymnasium, dance hall, and many other buildings –most spectacularly a two story, two-thirds of a mile-long enclosed track that provided for bicycles on the upper deck, and for riding horses on the lower deck.

Also, he had tennis courts built, and a field for a sport that was becoming America's pastime -baseball- using the track as its enclosure. And he added an opera house, which brought the country's most popular entertainments of the time, vaudeville and melodrama, to the 'Valley' for the first time. Mr. Sinclair had certainly created a competitive challenge to the French Lick Springs Hotel.

WEST BADEN SPRINGS OPERA HOUSE

Opera House Interior

West Baden Springs Hotel Enclosed Bicycle Track

PHOTOS FROM THE CLAY W. STUCKEY COLLECTION

UPS AND DOWNS

But the French Lick Springs Hotel had its champions. In the Gay 90s, as people were coming by train into town in record numbers, a traveler described the French Lick Hotel this florid way:

> *Nestled in the Hoosier hills, carpeted with green velvet grass, robed in the emerald of historic oaks and beeches and maples, canopied by orange and vermillion summer-day clouds and domed with the azure of a semitropical sky, this notable virgin spot, like a bride in all her wedding splendor dressed stands kissing her hand and smiling a welcome to the weary and careworn of the nation and the Earth. Across the ocean, at Carlsbad and Baden Baden, you can hear of the French Lick and West Baden Springs. Wherever the sands of life have run low, wherever care has begotten ill health, despondency and melancholy and the feverish fancy of suicide, the news of this great water fans into the flames and spark of hope, and like a magnet draws the patient hither to worship at nature's great shrine.*

But, as we all know, into each life a little rain must fall: First the Pluto Water stopped flowing in 1897. Because the springs were not only the symbol of the hotel, but also its greatest source of revenue, the very existence of the hotel came under jeopardy. Then, tragedy struck again. Within three weeks, the gorgeous, and deeply-loved-by-all-who-went-there, Windsor Hotel (the major structure on the grounds at the time), burned to the ground. This catastrophe, with the other attendant problems, caused those in charge to wonder if the hotel could continue. But, by sheer determination, the people of the hotel got together and resolved to save it.

First, fortunately, Windsor Hotel was almost totally covered by insurance, and this provided an incentive for more buildings. Secondly, the wells were dry because of a summer drought, and started back to normal within a few weeks (even though the hydrogen sulphide [fizz] was at a low level). It was also a time that many came to Springs Valley for entertainment.

VAUDEVILLE

A few years after Sinclair built his opera house, there was a boom in entertainment across America. Most communities around the country built at least one 'vaudeville' house, and some had 'opera' houses that were there for traveling opera companies, made popular by the great fame of Jenny Lind, the European opera star brought to America by P.T. Barnum, earlier in the century. (The appearance of opera star Jenny Lind around the country became so popular that tickets had to be distributed by a lottery draw.) Traveling 'Vaudeville' shows, which were entertainments with a variety of different 'acts,' started including brief appearances of opera singers.

MELODRAMAS

But in the last part of the century what emerged as the most popular entertainment in the country was the melodrama, where audiences were invited to cheer the hero and hiss the villain. The most famous melodrama of all, with characters based on a family living in Indiana, was "Uncle Tom's Cabin," written by Harriet Beecher Stowe, and performed over and over across the country.

After interviews with old timers remembering the West Baden Springs Hotel in the early 20th Century, Father John W. O'Malley writes:

> *In the evenings the hotel tried to offer diversified entertainment. The Opera House was open from fall to spring, and sponsored shows such as* What Happened to Jones *and* The Banker's Child, *or perhaps one of the Schubert comedies advertised as "clean and really humorous … a sensational terpschicorean novelty." During the summer months traveling drama companies pitched their tents inside the bicycle track area on the grounds.*
>
> *The Kritchfield Company would present its production of* Uncle Tom's Cabin. *A hotel guest would have the distinct privilege of watching "the best Tom, the cutest Eva, the funniest Topsy," all at the nominal cost of twenty five cents for adults and fifteen cents for children.*

Melodramas (which preceded movies, radio and television) featured stock characters, cliff hanger plots, and simple themes of good and evil. Their popularity was so great that cities small and large often had numerous theaters usually performing to packed houses. So it was not surprising that Mr. Sinclair built his own opera house, which featured melodramas that were touring the country. One of the melodramas featured scenes set in the West Baden Springs Hotel itself - which, of course, brought the swiftly evolving West Baden Hotel to the attention of theatergoers across the country. For guest entertainment at West Baden, many evenings were highlighted by a ball. By the late 1890s it looked like West Baden Springs Hotel was set to win the competitive battle with French Lick Springs Hotel. But looking to the north in Indianapolis, a young politician named Tom Taggart had his eye on French Lick.

Tom Taggart

The tale of Tom Taggart is a 'great American dreams-come-true' story. He was born in 1856 in County Manyhan, Ireland, and when he arrived with his parents in 1861, they settled in Ohio, and were part of the largest migration of the 19th Century –from famine-struck Ireland to the America-of-great-hope. Taggart's father was somehow able, much like John F. Kennedy's grandfather in Boston at about the same time, to develop a business of his own. The senior Taggart opened an Ohio restaurant which became very successful. This success made it possible to open a string of restaurants that reached over into Indianapolis, Indiana, and by 1876, the 20-year-old son, Tom, had shown enough promise to be put in charge of a number of them.

Within a few short years, young Tom Taggart became so popular and successful around Indianapolis that he decided to try his luck at politics. In 1886, he ran for Marion County Auditor, against an opponent who was on the unbeatable Republican ticket. The now 30-year-old Taggart possessed a fantastic memory of names. He would hear a name, or see a face, once, and remember it forever. This brought him hundreds of "friends," and he easily won the '86 election. Two years later he was even elected Marion County Democratic Chairman. In his new position, Taggart was able to parlay 'fees' from his job into a $50,000 a year job (by today's standards multiply by 20, at least). So suddenly, he found himself a young man with a fortune, and political power. This gave him a wide open field, and by 1890, as a vote getter, he actually outdid the President of the United States in his home county. By 1892, as the most popular politician in the state, he was named State Chairman of the Democratic Party, and the future was his oyster.

The now famous Tom Taggart virtually eased into being elected Mayor of Indianapolis in 1895.

The Grand Hotel, which Taggart owned, was an Indianapolis gathering place and a watering hole for politicians, and people of power in the 1890s, and Taggart used it to wield his influence. His accomplishments as mayor for six years included turning the developing frontier city of Indianapolis into a modern, efficient, metropolis, complete with parks, sewer system, and an overall responsive city government. He became known as the 'new organizer' and 'shaper for progress.' Then after his third term as a very successful mayor, he declined to run for re-election, and the city went back to the Republicans.

It was likely that Taggart's good-time success with the Grand Hotel in Indianapolis caused him to become interested in French Lick Springs Hotel with two partners, Crawford Fairbanks who owned a brewery, and L.T. Dickens, owner of an extensive Indiana Stone Quarry, who bought 80 acres of land near the hotel, and, after making plans with the owners of the Monon Railroad about new, more efficient ways of transportation, subscribed to $100,000 worth of bonds to build a third resort in French Lick. Then Taggart approached the board of owners of French Lick Springs Hotel, and told them his plans. After realizing the circumstance, they decided to sell, rather than compete with a third hotel in town. In 1901, the hotel property was merged to the French Lick Springs Hotel Company with Tom Taggart as president. Immediately Taggart made plans to double the size of his hotel to outdo the competition from Sinclair's hotel next door.

Incorporating Members, 1901
Crawford Fairbanks, L.T. Dickens, Tom Taggart

THE GREAT FIRE

Just as the fierce competition between Taggart and Sinclair was about to begin, tragedy struck. A spectacular fire, the worst in the history of the area, quickly leveled most of Mr. Sinclair's menagerie of buildings at West Baden Springs Hotel.

O'Malley describes the scene as recounted by eye witnesses:

> *Early in the morning of June 14, 1901, a fire broke out in the kitchen and within minutes raced through the dry, old wood of the West Baden Hotel. Fire and terror suddenly snatched the hotel into their grasp. Fortunately, no life was lost, even though the Chicago Daily Tribune's first story claimed that 200 people had lost their lives.*
>
> *The loss was greater than $500,000.*

Area people came to somberly look on the smoldering remains, presuming this was the end of the hotel for good. The opera house and the bicycle track were among the few buildings left standing. The community was in shock, and the employees, in large part, worried that their lives would never be the same again.

Sinclair went to the French Lick Springs Hotel Company, and offered to sell his property, 'as is' after the fire, for $700,000. The French Lick Springs Hotel Company offered $600,000. The deal, unbelievably, fell through. Now what?

Then came one of those defining moments in the history of Springs Valley. At his darkest hour, Mr. Sinclair made a decision that shook the world: he decided to build a hotel like nothing that had ever been built on planet earth, and he would complete it within a year since the fire. Most spectacularly, the centerpiece would be a great free standing dome, larger than any ever built. In West Baden Indiana!

The sheer audacity of constructing a dome larger than St. Peter's-- in a small town in Southern Indiana, and in less than a year-- was enough to suggest to his friends and associates that "he'd gone mad."

The Architecture of the Dome

Sinclair chose the dome structure, which has its own unique history. The dome is one of the major accomplishments in the history of architecture. For instance, the Pantheon built in 2nd Century AD Rome is still considered one of the great structures in the world. Even before the Pantheon, domes were considered a spectacular architectural feature. In Mesopotamia for instance, many were built, but because of the weakness in material, they didn't stand up, and are only known to us today through artistic renderings. It was the Byzantines of the 6th Century AD who first perfected the strong support system for domes and then on up through the Renaissance, the domes of St. Peter's in Rome, and St. Paul's in London, became iconic symbols for whole generations, and beyond.

Mr. Sinclair's audacious decision to build the world's largest free-standing dome called for great logistical coordination, and highly skilled people to pull it off.

For an architect, Sinclair chose Harrison Albright, who had been the West Virginia State architect. He was chosen likely because of his innovative work with domes, and reinforced concrete, which also fulfilled Sinclair's desire to build with a material that was "100 percent fire proof." For a builder, he chose Caldwell and Drake of Columbus Indiana, and gave them a financial incentive to get the work done in record time.

Soon work was underway. And the sight of hundreds of laborers rushing about has often been compared to what it must have been like when the pyramids in Egypt were constructed. Day by day huge progress was made. And sure enough the project was completed in less than a year! Mr. Sinclair even had guests at the new hotel with whom to celebrate his success, right on schedule. Many people called the feat "a miracle."

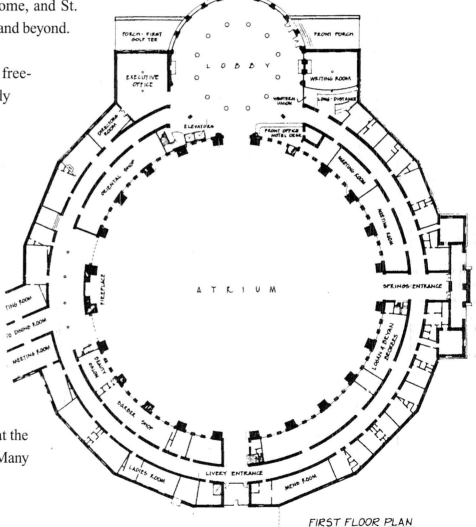

FIRST FLOOR PLAN

The Eighth Wonder of the World

Again, O'Malley, with early interviews of old timers who were there, described the incredible building…

The new hotel had an outer circumference of 1,010 feet. The inner rooms formed a perfect circle around the Pompeian Court and rose in circular tiers to the height of six stories. There were 708 rooms, each guest room being supplied with bath, lavatory, telephone, hot and cold water, steam heat, and electric lights. The Pompeian Court and dome, however, were the hotel's most striking and unique features. The dome was two hundred feet in diameter, and six hundred feet in inner circumference, and was a hundred and thirty feet high. The hub of the drum and the big dome was itself ten feet high, sixteen feet in diameter, and weighed eight and one-half tons. From the hub of the dome twenty-four ribs of steel, each weighing four and one-half tons, radiated to the pillars which supported them. Later a pavement of over twelve million marble mosaics would be laid in an intricate and beautiful design, and a wainscoting of Hauteville marble twelve feet high would cover the façade of brick.

The hotel's day of formal christening came on April 16, 1903. Overcast and chill after three days of steady rain the day dawned glorious nonetheless. Eight large American flags flew triumphantly in the breeze form atop the Moorish towers, and this octet was fittingly crowned by an enormous flag flying from atop the dome of the Pompeian Court. The hotel swarmed with dignitaries and sightseers. Ceremonies began at 2:30 in the afternoon with speeches in the Court, as Governor Winfield T. Durbin and Senator Charles W. Fairbanks marveled, wondered, and exclaimed with delight.

Governor Durbin's address, an elaborate eulogy of Sinclair, was typical of the event and the times:
' I myself wrote him a letter on the subject, in which I used every argument I could possibly employ to convince him of the hazards involved in this plan. Afterwards had a personal interview with him along the same line ... He told me in that interview that practically every friend he had in the world was opposed to his project, but that in spite of all opposition he was determined to go on.'

The keynote had been struck. A dream had come true. *The Journal*, in its quaint Victorian way, caught the spirit of the hotel's resurrection as well as anyone:

The new West Baden stands today, risen like a Phoenix from the ashes of despair to the very acme of its olden joy. The new hotel building of the West Baden Springs Company might very properly be called the "Eighth Wonder of the World."

CARLSBAD OF AMERICA

Mr. Sinclair's "Carlsbad of America," as he called his West Baden Hotel, became more famous nationally, and around the world. Sinclair's hotel published its own *West Baden Journal* - which was also the town paper. In 1902 the *The Journal* wrote that the hotel was not "patterned after any historical structure," and "the original designs indicate that Sinclair himself was responsible for the design of the extraordinary Eighth Wonder of the World."

The entertainment at West Baden on many evenings was highlighted by a ball. One of the more popular was the yearly St. Patrick's Day Ball in the atrium. It would be held in the evening after the afternoon parade through town. One West Baden Hotel flyer announced that "all Irish patriots (sex or color no bar) are cordially invited to visit the annual Ball of the Sons of Erin. (Ladies must not appear in green bloomers. Gentlemen must wear more than their complexion.)"

Visitors to the hotel often wondered what drove Sinclair to build his spectacular hotel as he did. Some have speculated that when Sinclair earlier visited Europe he was so impressed with the great domes he saw, that it was an easy decision for him to make.

Whatever the reason, the great dome in West Baden caught the attention of the world.

Part Two

The Glory Days of Two Grand Hotels in Springs Valley

The Brown Hotel which housed the biggest gambling enterprise in Springs Valley.

Enter A Third Entrepreneur

In the early 20th Century, Sinclair and Taggart, with their grand hotels famous for mineral springs, decided to emphasize another element to entice guests to Springs Valley: gambling. Although gambling was illegal it took a careful look-the-other-way culture of tacit approval from the governor's office, and a young brilliant entrepreneur named Charles "Ed" Ballard to make it all work.

Born a few miles west of French Lick in 1874, Ballard, as a boy, was a pinsetter at the West Baden hotel's bowling alley, and helped deliver laundry his mother washed for guests at West Baden Springs Hotel, and was soon delivering area mail on horseback. While still a teenager, Ballard worked at, then owned, a bar where he set up back room poker games, even though his mother was so opposed to gambling that she would not allow a deck of cards in her house. Soon Ballard also owned the Dead Rat Saloon, directly across the street from the West Baden Springs Hotel, which developed a large clientele of gamblers to raise capital. And for purchasing real estate and creating new business, young Ballard found ways to negotiate loans from local merchants which he would promptly repay. Sinclair soon invited Ballard to run his West Baden Casino, which he did while keeping his other enterprises going.

After Sinclair's hotel burned down in 1901, the 26-year-old Ballard was asked by Taggart to oversee the various gambling connections he directly had a hand in. Ballard took the job, which included running the biggest gambling enterprise in the valley, the Brown. Within three years Ballard owned the Brown and the most real estate and land in the area. He became a millionaire before turning thirty years old. And the gambling profit kept rolling in.

New Era

Mr. Sinclair's great accomplishment did not go unnoticed by the leader of the rival hotel. Taggart had made the French Lick Springs Hotel so successful that he bought out his partners. Within three years his debts had been paid. And he set into motion the largest rebuilding program the hotel had ever gone through.

The first major addition was a six story annexation of rooms on the south side; the bath house was then added to, and the power house enlarged. The three 'spring houses' (Pluto, Bowles, and Proserpine) were all rebuilt, and even a whole new floor of rooms was added atop the existing hotel. Largest of all, a new six floor main building faced with new yellow brick to match the old, was built, on the very spot the old Windsor Hotel had stood. These buildings were now all combined into one, making it a large grand hotel. Once completed, the new building program undertaken by Taggart had virtually doubled the size of the hotel space for guests. And with its new fire prevention material and construction techniques, it was called one of the safest and most luxurious hotels in the world.

DASTARDLY DEEDS

But the control of the water could be up for grabs. Taggart, in melodramatic fashion, early on faced a problem from an unlikely direction. Three former owners, John C. Howard, George S. Gagnon, and John L. Howard dug wells on the property adjoining the hotel, and lo and behold hit the underground stream that fed Pluto's Well. (It was later determined they were doing it basically for spite –and then blackmail.) This simply lowered the water pressure enough so that Pluto's Well no longer functioned. The water pumped up from the underground source by the men amounted to half a million gallons a day, and it was wasted into a nearby creek. One of them claimed, "I will sink old Pluto to hell (if) they don't take me back in or buy me out at my figures." Taggart took them to court which determined that because the men were wasting so much water, there had to be malice aforethought. Taggart won.

Then, in 1904, as Taggart had set up office as Democratic National Chairman in New York City, his secretary put up a display in the office lobby proclaiming the virtues of Pluto Water, and advertised the amenities of the hotel. Many New York newspapers printed scathing stories claiming Taggart was using his political position to enhance his business. This adverse publicity plagued Taggart personally. But the notoriety simply brought more business to the haven of Pluto's Well. Taggart 'won' again.

THE RIVALRY

While the rivalry between the hotels continued, there was also a rivalry among the patrons. Several people gave testimonies as to which hotel had the best curative waters. Mr. CL Pratt of Chicago wrote.

West Baden waters, beyond a doubt, for all chronic troubles, are the best in America, and if all the poor sufferers knew the truth as I do, the hillsides would be covered with the multitudes. Our fifty ailments, ranging from 'alcoholism to sterility' could be solved by benefiting from the waters. Two or three glassfuls before breakfast, three or four glasses in the forenoon, and a like quantity in the afternoon –followed by a brisk walk, not too tiring to aid the action of the waters.

But there was one circumstance where a rivalry did not obtain: In 1895, the West Baden Water Company, which could have competed with Pluto, was declared "unprofitable" by Sinclair and was closed down. Pluto Water, on the other hand, continued to be sent as 'bottled water' around the country by the train load.

THE RAID

As Taggart became more and more known on a national level, he began to face a lot of adverse publicity. For instance, when he opposed William Randolph Hearst's drive for the 1904 Democratic nomination for president, Hearst's national newspaper chain charged: "Tom Taggart conducts the greatest gambling hotel in America." A Hearst reporter claimed, "I saw all kinds of gambling –faro, roulette, poker, Klondike, the 'ponies,' books on the races, slot machines, etc. I saw a man and a woman gambling together!" Indiana Governor Hanley, a friend of Hearst's who opposed both gambling and the consumption of alcohol, had the state of Indiana bring suit against both Taggart and Sinclair for operating 'Gambling Hotels,' and raided the casinos. Taggart claimed he had nothing to do with gambling, and that "others" had leased the building used for gambling. A trial was held at the Orange County Courthouse in Paoli, and Judge Buskirk ruled in favor of the defendants, Tom Taggart and Lee Sinclair. And soon Springs Valley was back to 'normal' as if nothing had happened.

HOTEL AND TOWN

With profits at both hotels still on the rise and large rebuilding programs still underway, it appeared that the rivalry between Sinclair and Taggart was softened due to mutual success. While Sinclair remained a beloved local leader (two decades older than Taggart), Taggart was considered more of a national political figure. But despite many negative press stories about his politics, Taggart gained a reputation for being a kind-hearted, considerate, father figure by his employees, perhaps to compensate for the fact that they were not paid very well. He took an interest in their family problems, and took good care of them during sickness and trouble. He remembered all their names, a habit carried from his political career, and would often fold a gift dollar bill in a hand as he shook it. Sinclair, usually seen strolling the grounds with one of his beloved dogs, was a grandfather figure, still famous for creating the "Eighth Wonder of the World."

By 1904, Taggart had sold his Grand Hotel in Indianapolis, and now devoted himself to concentrating fully on his French Lick hotel, and the town itself. He contributed, first, a railway line between the two hotels in town –a mile-long-route streetcar for which the town fathers had happily voted to grant Taggart a right of way. Fares were five cents, and the rail line was totally first class. Sinclair welcomed the convenience of the rail line as mutual cooperation seemed to be setting in. Employees and guests from both hotels used it, and it ran from November 1903 to July 1919, finally being ousted by the production-line automobile-which was changing traveling habits throughout the country.

Sinclair also built a church for the local townspeople. Taggart provided electricity to the town from his own plant at the hotel. He erected poles, had wire strung, and that tiny Indiana town had electrical power years before most of the nation had electrical power. Thanks to the two grand hotels, Springs Valley became a delightful place in which to live.

A Turning Point

When President Teddy Roosevelt, at the turn of the 20th Century began challenging big business' unethical practices, he was called a 'trust buster' by demanding that protecting the rights of ordinary citizens took precedence over the self-interest of capitalists. This caused a major reassessment by the public on maters such as 'truth-in-advertising.' Soon health claims such as the curative powers of mineral water were also brought into question –which became a concern for both Taggart and Sinclair.

Widespread press coverage began when newspaper writers began doing more investigative reporting that challenged many of the verities that people had believed in for years. At the core of it all was a simple question: What is true and what should we believe?

This kind of questioning, however, was not new to America. Thomas Jefferson had said, a century earlier, that for a democracy to work, it needed an 'enlightened citizenry.' As it happened, the country's foray into 'public education' greatly increased the literacy rate in America, and newspaper reading and sales went through the roof. The citizenry had certainly become 'enlightened.' So it was not a surprise that by 1908 the intention of government and business began to be scrutinized more than ever. Charges by aggressive journalists called 'Muckrakers,' (such as those in John Bunyan's novel, *Pilgrim's Progress*, who "raked up the muck" that had gone unseen) became common. They claimed to be protecting the public by unearthing fraud and corruption.

Soon journalists were questioning the many health claims of advertised products, which caused the creation of the Pure Food and Drug Act, and meat inspection requirements. All this brought new awareness to the American public about non-scientific based health claims.

President Theodore Roosevelt

The great claims of the curative powers of mineral waters at Springs Valley were cut back, but many diehards still claimed the water's curative effects were real for them, scientific or not. Pluto Water continued to be a favorite American drink, even though its major claim was as an aid to digestion: "When nature won't, Pluto will."

FINISHING TOUCHES

Taggart seemed always to be putting 'finishing touches' on his hotel, as if to impress his steady flow of national political leaders, and the rich and famous who visited the hotels. In less than two years he added:

- a complete dairy barn with herds of cattle
- elegant porch additions
- a new pump house
- a golf house
- a shelter house
- improvements at the printing office
- additional green house
- elevator enclosures
- bath house enclosures
- lobby additions
- a laundry
- a bakery
- a 'water' building

Politicians from all over the country went back home and spread the good word, as the ever-proud Tom Taggart worked to beautify not only the hotel, but also the entire grounds.

A PICTURE OF FRENCH LICK SPRINGS

The grounds were kept immaculate, with flowered walks, bridal paths, and manicured lawns. The lawns had been created with tons of loam shipped in, to avert the springtime flooding that became a fairly regular occurrence in the area. But most especially, the grounds around the Monon Railway Station were kept beautiful, so that arriving patrons would instantly see the elegance as the train stopped. One patron remarked: "It was heaven on earth."

Rows of electrically lighted lamps dotted the outdoor areas, creating a Currier and Ives atmosphere. It was truly a fairy tale come to life in little French Lick, Indiana.

THE CHAIRMAN OF THE NATIONAL DEMOCRATIC PARTY

Inevitably, with French Lick Springs Hotel running successfully, Taggart began to put more emphasis on politics. He was surprised to find that although he had been out of elective office, the Taggart name and reputation had actually grown.

Taggart's national prominence began to rise when as a national committee man, he had the Indiana Convention push for Judge Alton B. Parker for President. Parker was unsuccessful, but at the end of the convention, the National Committee voted Taggart as Chairman of the Democratic Party. Taggart returned home to Indiana to a hero's welcome: their native son was suddenly one of the most prominent politicians in the country.

Next, Taggart moved into the National Headquarters offices in New York City, and took up his new duties. He immediately started an enormous push for Parker in the presidential race against Teddy Roosevelt. Well, as history would have it, the extraordinarily popular Roosevelt was elected President. Undeterred, Taggart, in 1908 (still the Democratic Chairman), threw his weight behind John W. Kern, also from Indiana, for Vice Presidential candidate under William Jennings Bryant. But in the general election, along came William Howard Taft to capture the election.

In 1912 it was a different story. Taggart was instrumental in a major shift in U.S. political history. At the Democratic Convention he pushed for the nomination of Indiana's Governor, Thomas Marshall, but after a long deadlock and 30 ballots, he switched his weight to newcomer Woodrow Wilson. Taggart, as National Chairman, then influenced other states to switch to Wilson for President, and Governor Marshall for Vice President. The convention went wild. Of course, Wilson and Marshall went on to win the election in the fall of 1912, and beyond that prove to create one of the most important administrations in 20th Century politics.

Wilson, the gentleman scholar from the East, and Marshall, the governor of the bustling mid-Western state, Indiana, were able to get legislation behind an initiative that led to 'hope-for-peace,' a plan for a 'League of Nations.' Years later, Wilson's ideas, far ahead of their time, were largely inculcated into the UN Charter. Mr. Taggart's powers of persuasion and influence had again shown results.

The rivalry between Taggart and Sinclair became a national story of interest, and even included a bit of a contest to see who could get the biggest named celebrities as guests at their respective hotels. It was also just about the same time that claims were made that Springs Valley and Saratoga Springs in New York were now considered the most heralded escapes to visit in America. Two to three times an hour packed carloads of guests arrived at the French Lick train station ready to have a few days of fun.

Because of the overflow crowds at the two grand hotels, many smaller hotels kept popping up. These hotels, of many shapes and sizes, could house 25 to 300 guests each, and ranged in cost from $1.00 to $3.00 a day. A Monon rail line publication claimed that almost 3,000 guests a day could be accommodated –a number substantially larger than the local population. The quality of the accommodations also had a wide range, but everyone seemed to benefit –from the Monon Railroad line to the many gambling establishments in town.

Hotels in Springs Valley

Arlington Hotel	French Lick Springs Hotel	Oxford Inn
Avenue Hotel	Grigsby House	Perrin House
Burton House	Grand Hotel	Ritter House
Claxton Hotel	Homestead Hotel	Ryan Hotel
City Hotel	Hotel Pavilion	Sutton Hotel
Colonial Hotel	Hotel Windsor	Toliver Hotel
Ellis House	The Howard	The Wells Hotel
Erwin Hotel	Lindley Inn	West Baden Springs Hotel

Casinos in Springs Valley

Also Springs Valley had more than a dozen gambling establishments at any one time, where bets could go up to $50,000 a hand. These 'clubs' had names that ranged from the 'Dead Rat Club' to the 'Elite Café.' And many had at least an indirect connection to a "house of ill repute" or two.

Babylon Club
The Brown
Colonial Club
Club Chateau
Dead Rat Club
Elite Café
French Lick Springs Hotel (early on)
The Gorge
Green Acres Casino
Indiana Club
Kentucky Club
Oxford Hotel
Ritter House
Round Tree Inn
Sutton House
West Baden Springs Hotel (early on)

Gambling Establishments

The gambling establishments varied from the out-in-the-open, to hard-to-find, from back-room to the up-the-outside stairway, to full establishments such as The Brown, and the 'high rollers' had their favorites here and there. The locals were not invited to most of the 'clubs' because a local pay check could be lost on gambling within minutes. But many hotel employees could give 'tips' to the novice or the high roller --for a small fee!

Gamblimg

Archeological finds and historical records reveal that people have gambled since the beginning of recorded history. Gambling implements such as early versions of dice have been found among the oldest of civilizations –China, India, and Egypt going back to at least 3000 BC. And up through much of western civilization, beginning with the ancient Greeks and the Romans, gambling in one form or another, even betting on who could pitch a coin closest to the wall, has been pervasive. The European courtiers bet on hawking and bear baiting in the Renaissance and over time a variety of 'sporting' events have been rife with betting all around the world --for small and large stakes-- right down to modern times.

While over the years there have been fierce battles over the morality of gambling, in recent times governments themselves have gotten involved and have made gambling more acceptable with their state controlled lottery revenues being earmarked for education and other social needs. Some claim that the urge to gamble reaches into many of the things we do, whether it's today's stock market, or the natural risks in life we take day-to-day. Obviously the 'lure' is stronger in some than in others.

In Springs Valley, the lure of gambling at least matched the lure of mineral waters as the major enticement that brought patrons to the grand hotels. The 'escapes' to French Lick Springs Hotel and West Baden Springs Hotel --although blessed with the beauty of nature, entertainment, sports, and other amenities that brought peace of mind and relaxation-- were made possible by a roll of the dice.

 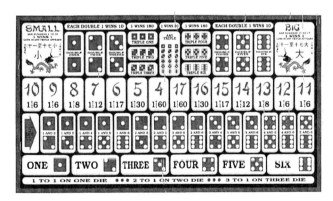 

Left: betting on a Medieval form of Backgammon.
Above: "Sic Bo," an antique dice pairing game, still popular today.
Right: ancient Asian silk and oil-paper playing cards

Springs Valley Gambling

Many say that the Springs Valley Casinos were the Las Vegas of the early part of the 20th Century. It is true that from early on, the mere mention of French Lick meant gambling. And it annoyed Tom Taggart no end. He saw himself as an upright, religious, family man setting an example for a son and five daughters he loved dearly. And he often proclaimed, he didn't drink or smoke, and from the beginning argued that drinking and gambling on the property were definitely not part of the hotel's amenities. But Mr. Taggart benefited mightily from the many gambling establishments within walking distance of his hotel.

Mr. Sinclair, on the other hand briefly established the West Baden casino without apologies. Certainly when he hired Ballard in 1895 there was no doubt that he saw there was big money to be made in gambling.

Early on, Al Brown & Associates along with a number of other local operators had been arrested for running cards and games. All had pleaded guilty in local courts –and paid fines. Then things went back to normal. In 1903, the State Attorney General had begun investigating the casino gambling in French Lick, but fortunately for Taggart, Thomas Marshall, his friend, became governor, and the investigation was slowed. However, due to the controversy, Taggart had Brown and his casino thrown off the property. Brown straightaway built a new building across the street using the same yellow brick as the hotel's, as well as the same architect. And his new casino was reported to be connected with reputed nearby houses of prostitution. The building looked like it was a part of French Lick Springs Hotel, and there are reliable claims that Taggart allowed Brown to hook up to the hotel's heating system. The hotel and Brown began drawing more people than ever.

ORGANIZED CRIME

In 1906, members of a Chicago mob arrived in French Lick. It was organized crime wanting in on the action making demands for 'protection' money from both Taggart and Sinclair. When both refused, the mobsters dynamited the veranda at the French Lick Monte Carlo, and the 'gaming room' at West Baden Springs Hotel. It looked like a major turf war was about to begin. There were rumors that a deal was cut, just before the mobsters left town, not to return. But the two hotel owners stood their ground and refused to be intimidated. All evidence suggests that the outside mob was successfully resisted, and gambling stayed under local 'control.'

Taggart continued to claim that he didn't gamble and that he didn't like gambling. But he knew that the lure of gambling brought large crowds to his hotel and made it successful. It was later discovered he received up to $50,000 a year as a piece of the action.

HEARST ATTACKS BALLARD

At the time of Taggart's battle with Hearst over politics and gambling in 1904-06, Ballard's gambling establishments also came under fierce attack. First Hearst's newspapers attacked Ballard in editorials decrying gambling in French Lick:

Newspaper tycoon William Randolph Hearst

Ed Ballard, a gambler born and raised in West Baden, is the gentleman who pulls the very Luscious chestnuts out of the fire for Mr. Taggart. Mr. Ballard pays Mr. Taggart $50,000 a year for the gambling privilege at French Lick Hotel. A few years ago he was working for $6 a week. Now he is worth a reported $200,000.

Entrepreneur Charles "Ed" Ballard

James Fadely in his excellent biography *Thomas Taggart* (1997) writes:

> *In spite of his success up to this point Ballard was now experiencing rough times with his casino businesses. Gov. Jefferson Davis of Arkansas had just closed down Ballard's Arkansas Club at Hot Springs, and Hearst's crusade had resulted in closing his casino in Santa Barbara, California, as well. Ballard also had a casino in Los Angeles and was reportedly interested in setting up business in eastern resort areas. The Springs Valley raid could not have come at a worse time for the likable, big-hearted Ballard.*

But Ballard was able to breeze on through the bad press, and his enterprises all continued to grow.

Meanwhile *The New York World* called on Taggart to resign as Democratic National Chairman, but he refused to do it, claiming the attacks on him and his hotel were "personal."

PLUTO PLANT

Taggart's Pluto Water empire continued to grow. A spectacular new building was constructed in 1913 that brought a horde of visitors to it. It was a new Pluto Processing Plant. Taggart decided that a 'processing' plant was necessary, "to make the water more appetizing to drink." Sparing no cost and using up-to-date technology and ideas, Taggart developed a 'new brew.' It was an instant success. Soon Pluto Water became a household name in America, as many more train car-loads were daily shipped to destinations across the land, bringing millions of dollars back to the sole owner, Taggart himself. Also, each bottle was a small advertisement for the French Lick Springs Hotel.

PROCESSING PLUTO WATER

Here is how the processing of Pluto Water was explained in a pamphlet of the time:

> *The water as it flows from the spring was not in condition to be bottled or shipped. The gases contained in the water caused coloration and sediment to form when the water was bottled. The water acquired a disagreeable odor and made the water unfit for drinking purposes. To avoid these results the waters were first pumped directly from the spring to vats on the fifth floor of the bottling plant. Here they were bottled by use of steam coils. When boiled the gases were thrown off, and at the same time Epsom salts and glauber salts were added to the water. The boiling water dissolved these salts and held them in solution. Actually those two elements were already contained in the waters, but in this process the water was 'strengthened or fortified.' The water then passed to the fourth floor where it was cooled and clarified. On the floor below it was further cooled before being sent to the bottom floor bottling rooms where it was bottled, labeled and packed.*

A Mutually Beneficial Rivalry

By 1914, the two grand hotels made Springs Valley in Indiana arguably the most popular vacation escape in America. The rivalry between the two was the catalyst that drove much of the progress at both hotels. The amenities were growing at West Baden Springs Hotel, and the guests kept coming from far and wide for the mineral water, for strolling the grounds, for the ever more popular entertainment at the opera house, and simply to see the sheer grandeur of the huge dome and, of course, gambling. At French Lick Springs Hotel, the orchestra, the entertainment, and the many political events grew in size and frequency, and the long list of visiting notables grew larger.

Also, at West Baden, the guests included hundreds of celebrities from around the country, and countless politicians including the governors of Indiana and the surrounding states, and the mayors of many major cities around the country: Mayor "Big Bill" Thompson of Chicago, and Richard Crocker of New York's Tammany Hall, visited West Baden Springs Hotel.

Sports

For many years the sports world made the name 'West Baden Hotel' a household word. In the early days the first heavyweight champion, John L, Sullivan, James J. Corbett, and William Sharkey all visited or trained at the hotel, and later, there was the great champion Joe Louis, whose training location became a tourist stop. And golf and tennis at French Lick Springs Hotel became evermore popular.

But the sporting event that brought the most attention was baseball. Several major league teams, in the early days of professional baseball, held their Spring training at the West Baden 'diamond': the Chicago Cubs, the Pittsburgh Pirates, the Philadelphia Phillies, the St. Louis Cardinals, the Cincinnati Reds, the St. Louis Browns all had their day there. Major stars of the time such as Dizzy Dean were cheered by local fans. And on the off-times, 'pick up' teams representing the various Springs competed. For instance, Mayor Swift of Chicago captained the "Hats" of Spring #7 to victory over the "Colds" of #5. And a swell time was had by all.

Donald Ross, the most famous golf course architect in America at the time, built his spectacular "hill" course just west of Springs Valley and soon won such wide acclaim that it was picked to host the PGA Tournament won by the legendary Walter Hagen. The course was to become one of the favorites in the Midwest.

Two golf courses were built in Springs Valley. Thomas Bendelow, who built hundreds of golf courses around the country, constructed a 9 hole course at the turn of the century, called the Valley Course. In 1910 Bendelow rebuilt it as an 18 hole course.

In 1914, the 'Great' War, as it was first called, began in Europe and soon was raging trench to trench. America, while still not fighting in the war yet, became the major supplier of war material up to and during the US entry into World War I. Taggart, Sinclair, and Ballard kept Springs Valley buzzing along.

BEECHWOOD

Meanwhile, Beechwood, the "mansion" that Ballard built in 1914 for his wife, Dolly, and children, became the talk of the town, as the most lavish in the valley. In *The Ballards in Indiana* Ed Ballard's son Chad Ballard describes the home he once lived in:

Constructed of smooth red brick, the lovely home exhibited the quality workmanship of local craftsmen who took enormous pride in their work Fireplaces of imported marble arrived from France and Greece Fountains and statuary were purchased in Italy and the black walnut paneling came from Circassia on the Black Sea. Antique furniture, art objects, and paintings collected from all over the world graced the mansion. Adorning the music room was a custom built concert grand piano of hand painted bird's-eye maple which a good friend, Irving Berlin, enjoyed when visiting the home.

Ed's love of books was evident in his spectacular library which housed the literary classics of the ages. Custom leather bound, gold embossed, with gold leaf edges, the books provided joyful times for him, and a stranger observing the articulate, urbane gentleman could not have guessed he had left school at age 10 to set pins in a bowling alley. An Indiana University history professor said, 'I could have sworn he was a history professor!' Rollicking good times were had by the children and their many playmates for many activities centered around their happy home.

With Beechwood his new headquarters, set prominently in the middle of Springs Valley, Ballard was setting up to expand his empire, and become the richest and most powerful man in Springs Valley.

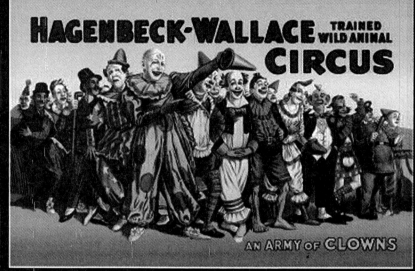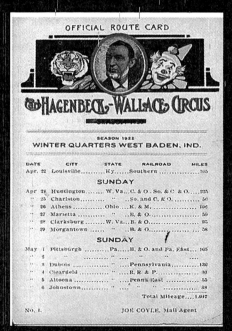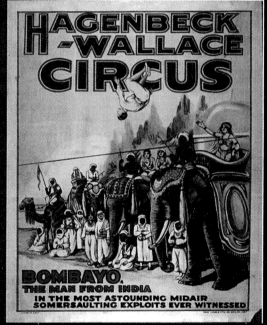

BALLARD'S CIRCUS ERA BEGINS

"The biggest event ever in Springs Valley history was when Ballard's circus came to town," claimed the local newspaper. But not only did it come to town –it stayed and made its winter headquarters there—with local-boy-made-good, the multimillionaire Ed Ballard at the helm. Soon many circus buildings covered the acres of land he had purchased nearby Beechwood, and during the outdoor season, the circus traveled all over the world. Within a few years, it grew into the largest circus in the world. Not since the old days of P.T. Barnum! Here's the story.

The first version of Ballard's circus actually began in Peru, Indiana in 1882, when livery stable owner Benjamin Wallace bought a bankrupt circus, hired entertainers from the best troupes, and set up on local land bought from the Miami Indians. Peru became a railroad hub by the early 20th Century, and was home to the growing, successful circus that merged with another successful pioneering circus founded by the extraordinary animal trainer, Karl Hagenbeck. Before long, their fame grew as the exceptional, exciting, and very popular Hagenbeck-Wallace Circus. It soon toured around America and received national acclaim. By 1913, however, in a flash flood on the Wabash River in Indiana, many of the animals were lost, and Wallace sold his interest in the circus. Within two years, the circus was principally owned by Ed Ballard, the casino gambling whiz. Ballard had begun reaching out beyond his gambling emporiums and now delighted in taking on a circus, and bringing it back to his hometown. The excitement in Springs Valley was palpable, and the *Springs Valley Herald* enthusiastically announced the news:

Springs Valley Herald –July 22, 1915
West Baden, Ind., July 10 – (Special)

Ed Ballard, who with C.E. Cory, controls the corporation which operates the Great Hagenbeck-Wallace Shows, accompanied by a landscape artist and architect, arrived here today and announced that the Hagenbeck-Wallace Company had chosen this city as the place where it would erect its big winter quarters and repair shop. The leading citizens were jubilant over the news, and a movement was promptly inaugurated to grant the big circus exemption from taxation for ten years. It also was planned by the people of the valley to raise a fund by subscription and with same to build one of several new buildings Mr Ballard is easily the most popular man in these parts and has turned down many alluring and attractive offers from other municipalities. West Baden feels highly complimented. Every citizen concedes that Mr. Ballard has treated the town handsomely and deserves handsome treatment in return.

The grooms, animal men, keepers, trainers, and mechanics in the repair shows will be carried through the winter and the population of the town will be increased to that extent.

Besides that the shows will rehearse and open here annually, and that means that the whole 500 employees will be here each spring for periods ranging from two to four weeks each. The money paid out in salaries will amount to huge sums and merchants and hotel men will benefit vastly.

The winter quarters, furthermore, will be a distinct acquisition as a show place and will be an added interest for the guest of the big hotels. It is planned to erect very beautiful buildings and to park the land all about them and make the site as attractive as artistry and ingenuity can.

Mr. Ballard's handsome home will not be greatly distant from the location chosen. This mansion, the most spacious and beautiful in the Valley, has also lent much class to the great American spa.

It is planned to 'tarvia' all roads and turnpikes centering at West Baden, thus providing many charming drives and excursions for automobile parties.

There is no evidence of hard times or tight money at West Baden. Money is being spent like water on improvements.

By the Fall the resort will be the most attractive in America, if not in the world.

Over the summer the excitement built, especially among the children. The skeptics in town were sure crowds wouldn't come to tiny French Lick and West Baden Indiana to see a circus. But overall there was great hope, and again, the local newspaper sang the praises in alliteration of how the "gayest, grandest, gladest galaxy" in all the wide world is coming on Saturday.

Springs Valley Herald
September 2, 1915
HAGENBECK-WALLACE
Ed Ballard's Big Show Coming
WILL BE HERE SEPTEMBER 11

Peanuts and pink lemonade will soon be ripe and the odor of sawdust tanbark will permeate the air. The Carl Haganbeck-Wallace Circus, gayest, grandest, gladest, galaxy in all the wide world is coming to French Lick and West Baden, Saturday, Sept. 11, for two performances, this year the big show, will come aboard three special trains, with many boxcars, the longest ever used to transport a circus aggregation. The country for miles around is all aglow with the noisy circus upon which thousands of eyes feast their gaze. Father Time is always on the job, scenes come and go, but somehow or other, the circus is just the circus and its popularity never wanes.

All through the long months of winter agents of the Hagenbeck-Wallace Shows have been scouring the continents of the earth securing novelties and features. The performances this year will be entirely new. More than three hundred acrobats, gymnasts, riders, contortionists and athletes together with fifty clowns compose the circus and, in addition the big show is augmented with Karl Hagenbeck's trained wild animal exhibition. Hundreds of wild animals, lions, leopards, tigers, pumas, jaguars, elephants, seals, monkeys, etc. will constitute that department.

Beneath the pomp and glitter and amidst the odor of sawdust and naphtha is a system of government and management whose scope and scale are stupendous and staggering. No human institution is more perfect in operation than the circus. Surely no more flattering tribute could be paid the Hagenbeck-Wallace Show than that officially given by the United States government. Officers from the army department carefully observed the rapid sequence of proceedings when the big show was in Washington.

The naval officers were in the railroad yards to watch the arrival of the trains, the process of debarkation, and of the show grounds they marveled at the manner in which the monster Aladdin like palaces were raised into the air. They critically observed the manner in which the two mile long street parade was lined up. They marveled at the haste and precision in which hundreds of their employees hastened ahead of their work.

Gen. Evans surveyed the marvelous scenes and he was dumbfounded. He asked Mr. Wallace to permit several members of his staff to travel with the

show a fortnight that they might grasp a few of the advanced ideas as to how so great an institution is moved with apparently so little effort. Gen. Evans confessed that the army department had always loaded their wagons on flat cars by hoisting them over the side, not rolling them from the end.

The Hagenbeck-Wallace Shows owned by Ed Ballard is the most wonderful circus organization in the world. The Hagenbeck-Wallace circus will come to French Lick and West Baden, Saturday, Sept. 11, for performances at 2 and 8 p.m. It will have on exhibition in the menagerie the smallest hippopotamus every brought to America. It reached the circus a few weeks ago, and has been given a place of honor among the many other unusual specimens of Far Eastern animal life. The river horse was caught in British South Africa by means of a pitfall –a deep trench, the mouth of which s covered by a network of moss and sticks to resemble the grassy earth. When the animal took his fatal plunge, he fought so ferociously that it required fifty natives to drag him from the dark hole and make a prisoner of him.

The children who visit the circus will be delighted when they see the two cutest little jungle babies, being captive-born lions. They are little

balls of soft fur with bright, blinking eyes and playful paws. Their mother, and a proud beast she is, watches over her offspring zealously. Woe be to the venturesome keeper who seeks to pet those babies through the bars of the cage.

One of the institutions on the Hagenbeck-Wallace circus grounds is the traveling post office. Probably no other office in America is visited daily by such a cosmopolitan gathering. Harvey Johnson is the postmaster. He is well fitted for the job, as he speaks French, German, Spanish, Hindostani and Polish and knows enough Chinese, Japanese, Portuguese and modern Greek to make himself understood in those tongues, spoken by the performers who hail from around the world.

An idea of the cosmopolitan aspect of the show may be had from a careful study of all the people in the morning parade. For an hour the wonders of the Earth unfold themselves as they pass before the spectators. There are dusky queens, seated in richly draped howdahs on the backs of elephants; desert chieftains, perched on camels and dromedaries; far eastern potentates and the retinues in golden chariots and thrones; Australian bushmen and boomerang throwers, on horses; the military of European kingdoms, richly costumed; court ladies and diplomats in coaches of state; Oriental statesmen in rickshaws and palanquins, and savage chiefs and tribesmen, in barbarian carriages of war. The characteristic music of the counties of the Earth is played by bagpipes, great brass bands, organs, reed and string orchestras, castanet ballets, tom-tom players, drum and bugle corps, weird changers, chimes and siren pipes. The circus has about 1,100 employees, 800 horses and menagerie animals. It travels on three trains and during the day time is housed in twenty-two tents covering 14 acres of ground. The show has its own light. In the canvas hotel thousands of meals are served everyday of the week.

Among the interesting features of this show is the Llama, an animal that in a very early period was worshiped by inhabitants of South America. Another animal of great interest is the River Horse--Hippopotamus. Its native home is the great rivers and lakes of Africa. It is a water animal, diving beneath when danger arises, but at internals raising its head above the surface to breathe. It feeds on the roots and barks of water trees and plants.

The Leopard, which was spoken of by the Prophet Isaiah, is another animal of the show that deserves your attention. This animal has been known from the earliest historical times, and probably the largest geographical range of the entire animal family. It is found throughout the African continent, the whole of south Asia, and in Ceylon, Java, Sumatra and Borneo. The Leopard is fierce and blood thirsty, and the fact that the Hagenbeck-Wallace circus has subdued this animal merits the attention of the student of Natural History.

Another feature of interest of this show is the Owl, not the hooting or screeching owl that we are all so familiar, but the Monkey Faced Owl, which is very unlike about two hundred species which are known. But to attempt to enter into detail or to try to speak of all the interesting things of the Hagenbeck-Wallace Circus would require much time, therefore, the thing to do is to spend a day at this circus, watch the procession to by, go into the show and see the great feats of horsemanship, the exhibits of acrobatic displays, and go home forgetting all the troubles you have ever had in your life! The Circus is owned by Mr. Ed Ballard.

The circus was a great success, and lived up to the colorful stories describing it in the *Springs Valley Herald*. The 14,000 people who attended on Saturday now had a lifetime of memories to tell and retell. Little did they know that the 41-year-old Ballard still had many more tricks up his sleeve, as he was fast becoming the new P.T. Barnum of America, based in tiny Springs Valley!

A few days after the event, the Springs Valley Herald weighed in:

Springs Valley Herald (September 16, 1915)
TEN THOUSAND
PEOPLE SEE BALLARD'S BIG SHOW SATURDAY AFTERNOON HERE
BIGGEST CROWD EVER HERE

French Lick and West Baden certainly gave Ed Ballard and his big show a cordial greeting here last Saturday. People began pouring into town at a very early hour and by ten o'clock and long before the street parade the streets of both towns were surging with humanity. A big excursion train bearing thousands of people came in over the Monon, and the Southern brought in excursions from its eastern and western division of the main line as well as the branches.

The big parade reached this city from West Baden at 10 minutes after 10 o'clock and was a magnificent pageant and was about a mile long. Mr. Sinclair of the West Baden Springs Hotel rode in the leading carriage with Mr. Ballard. The French Lick Springs Hotel Band also had a place in the parade and was well received from the thousands who knew the boys.

Immediately after the parade people began pouring into the big tent and at 2 o'clock every available seat was taken and still the eager stream came pouring in. 1000 folding chairs were brought in and these did not go halfway round the probably 2000 more that had to stand or sit on the ground.

At no place or any time this season has the big show simply been swamped with people.

We understand that part of the management were afraid to come here as they thought it would be a losing proposition, they perhaps feel different about it now.

It is estimated that 10,000 people saw the show in the afternoon and 4,000 at night.

It certainly had been an auspicious start, and Ed Ballard soon began looking for other circuses to buy. Meanwhile, as the era of Ballard was leaping forward, another era was about to come to an end.

The End of A Fairy Tale Life
at
Sinclair's West Baden Springs Hotel

Looking back over time, as Sinclair's health began deteriorating, his West Baden Springs Hotel had been a work in progress from the first time he became a principle owner. And in his declining years, he could look back over his accomplishments such as the beautiful opera house that presented the popular entertainment of the time, or the remarkable two story track, among many other amenities. He could reminisce about his crowning achievement that produced the "Eighth Wonder of the World." And how over the years, he added the gardens, stables, shops, baths, and even a hospital. Or how his visitors, from great distances came to see his remarkable domed architectural masterpiece. Sinclair loved that so many came away feeling better than before they got there –usually crediting the medicinal powers of the waters and the luxury of pure relaxation. In early 1916, Sinclair, his daughter Lillian and her husband Charles Rexford together agreed on a plan for yet another major renovation. But within months, in September 1916, with many countries in the world at war, the 80-year-old Lee Wiley Sinclair passed away.

People from far and wide, who began to realize how sizeable his accomplishments were, ventured to the huge atrium, under the great dome where the great innovator was laid in state. Eulogy after eulogy praised Sinclair's accomplishments, praising a long lifetime (1836-1916) during which the world had gone from a rural agrarian horse and buggy society to a modern world of technological wonder. 1,200 people attended the funeral in the grand atrium of the hotel. A special train carried the body, and funeral party, to Louisville where Sinclair was buried. However, the family mausoleum at Crown Hill Cemetery in Salem, Indiana, which now also holds his wife and daughter, also became the final resting place for Sinclair.

Meanwhile Lillian and her husband decided to continue the improvements on the hotel on their own, and just a few days after Sinclair's death, the *West Baden Journal* published a list of the outstanding features of Sinclair's 'eighth wonder of the world.' Here are some of those features:

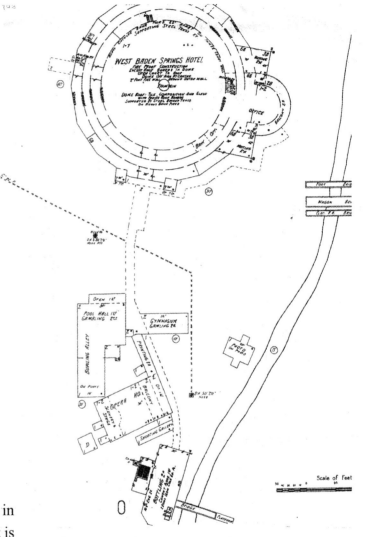

The hotel was designed in all its details by its owner, Hon. Lee W. Sinclair, but the plans were drawn by Harrison Albright of Charlestown, W.Va.

While the hotel may be called a combination of all schools of architecture, the prevailing style is Moorish.

The dome has the distinction of being positively the largest ever constructed in the world.

The floor space in the hotel, including the atrium is 15 acres. The air space in the atrium is 2,730,000 cubic feet.

1,275 car-loads of material were used in the construction of the building:
13 cars of stone;
16 cars of red brick,
26 cars of lime,
45 cars of steel,
51 cars of lumber;
62 cars of cement,
171 cars of gravel;
187 cars of sand;
242 cars of cinders,
450 cars of white brick.
12 cars of miscellaneous material

The building is octahedron in shape, 343 feet in diameter by 1,000 feet in circumference, and surmounted by the immense dome (about sixty feet is devoted to the curving crown of the dome). Eight million bricks were used in the construction.

The hub of the dome is 10 feet long and 16 feet in diameter and weighs eight and one half tons.

Each of the 24 steel ribs which stretch from the hub to the walls weighs four and one half tons. The total amount of steel in the hub is 120 and a half tons. The ribs rest on rollers on top of the supporting columns, thus providing for the expansion and contraction of the metal.

The only wood in the structure is contained in the door and window casings and in the ball room floor.

The outside of the hotel building measures 1,010 feet. The atrium has a circumference of 600 feet and a diameter of 200 feet.

The hotel contains 708 rooms, each of which is provided with a bath, lavatory, clothes closet, steam heat, electric lights, hotel and cold water and telephone.

The floors are composed of cement and iron and are 7 inches thick.

The glass dome if laid end to end would make a walk 16 inches wide and two and three quarter miles long.

The glass in the hotel if laid end to end would make a walk two miles long and thirty inches wide. There is more glass in the building than in any other building in the world, including the famous Crystal Palace in London.

The only other building in the world having a large dome constructed of steel, is the capital at Washington. It is only 128 feet in diameter, however, therefore much smaller. The great dome at St. Petersburg, which is the second largest in the world is only 160 feet in diameter or 40 feet less than the dome of the West Baden Springs Hotel.

The factor of safety of the dome is six. By this is meant the amount of weight it will sustain. If to the weight of the materials used in constructing the dome, there be added the weight of 18 inches of wet snow, covering its entire surface, and the total amount be multiplied by six, the product will represent be total weight as the case may be which the dome will sustain without breaking.

The dome is absolutely fire-proof.

ANOTHER FIRE!

Within a few months after Sinclair's death, on February 1917, there was another major fire at West Baden Springs Hotel. Two major fires in fifteen years! "It's a good thing the old man wasn't here to see it," said a long-time employee. This time not the main building, but major structures were ruined.

As reported at the time, with the weather hovering at zero degrees for a few days, the water 'plugs' were solidly frozen, and once the fire broke out in the new x-ray room in the West Baden Hospital, there was no stopping it as it swept the frame structures that connected the hospital, the opera house and the bowling alleys. It soon consumed the hot water parlor over Spring No. 7, and the bottling house. Fortunately, the main building was spared and there were no patients in the hospital at the time, and the large audience scheduled for the popular Vogel Minstrel Troupe at the opera house had not yet arrived. Despite the loss, Rexford and Lillian decided to keep the renovation going ahead.

Another Opening Gala

By October 1917, there was another grand opening, featuring the outside, modern spring 'houses,' replacing the wooden pagodas that marked an earlier time. There were new sunken gardens. Inside, intensive work was done on modernizing guest rooms, and the Atrium had a 'classical reformation' from floor to ceiling, featuring marble lower walls, and from a Grecian-like frieze design atop the dome, a matching pattern laid in the floor with 12 million one-inch square marble mosaic tiles gave the atrium a startling new look.

To 'watch over' this transformation: three muses, Calliope (the Muse of Epic Poetry), Thalia (the Muse of Comedy), and Clio (the Muse of History), and none other than the great Grecian God of Light, Music, Poetry, and Prophecy: Apollo. But the hotel was not the same anymore. With the growing war in Europe sapping much of the western world's travel and leisure time, the number of guests at West Baden Springs Hotel was greatly reduced, causing alarming financial problems. But somehow Rexford seemed to find the money for the extensive renovations. Lillian had to have sensed that there was something amiss, and her relationship to her husband, reportedly, was getting worse. And when Lillian was approached later in 1918 and asked to consider leasing the hotel for use as a US Army Hospital to house wounded US troops returning from the war, she jumped at the chance. But much in her marriage had already started to unravel.

Across America, 1918 was a year of grave health concerns. First, there was the great pandemic of Influenza that swept across the world leaving an estimated 17,000,000 dead. Called the Great Flu Epidemic, because it was so widespread, it filled hospitals in many places, and stretched health services severely. On top of that World War I was in full sway, and in Europe there were many millions of casualties —dead and wounded, that decimated the population of a generation of young men.

In June of 1918 the US sent its first expeditionary force under General John J. Pershing which joined the battles against the Germans and Austrians. Nearly a million US troops followed, and by the end of the war the terrible sacrifice of American armed forces was: 130,000 dead and missing, and over 200,000 wounded.

Army Hospital #35

Because medical facilities across the US were already over-stretched from the flu epidemic, when wounded American troops began arriving by the Fall of 1918, new facilities were sought after across the country to be put to use as US military hospitals. It was during this time that Lillian [Sinclair] decided that she would lease the West Baden Springs Hotel as US Army General Hospital #35.

Straightaway renovation for turning the building into a hospital got underway. Some of the same workers who helped Mr. Sinclair build the "Eighth Wonder of the World" sixteen years earlier were back at work, this time proudly doing a patriotic job. It was also during this time that Lillian discovered that her husband had been borrowing large sums of money for hotel renovations from none other than Ed Ballard, and her marriage in all but name was ended.

In November 1918, the wounded soldiers began arriving, and it became a very busy hospital. Now separated from her husband, Lillian stayed at the hotel, and took on the gratifying job of helping nurse the wounded soldiers back to health.

As for soldiers, the process of getting well in such elegant surroundings was a great lift to the spirits.

That Christmas Back Home

From a publication of US Army Hospital #35, *Under the Dome,* the recuperating soldier's experiences of that first Christmas 'home' are described by a hospital worker:

> *It may be of interest to know how Christmas 1918 was spent at this hospital. Just a year ago they were in the trenches and 'didn't even have a cigarette' Probably in no other place in the world could this be. First of all, the Atrium ... 135 feet high and 200 feet across, circular, and each floor has rooms with windows of the double French variety opening wide. All these windows were lined with patients. Those unable to walk either had their beds carried to the windows, or were rolled there in wheeled chairs, so as to see everything. The Atrium had been decorated with long streamers from the balconies on the top floor, gracefully curving 50 feet to a common center 50 feet from the floor ... Below was a 45-foot Christmas tree, artistically hung with festive bulbs, balls, etc., the star of the tree being lighted by electric bulbs after dark. The evening before each patient had been given a kit bag containing numerous good and handy articles.*
>
> *After breakfast on Christmas morning, games, walks, music from 3 pianos in different parts of the atrium and a phonograph for bed patients. After dinner everyone repaired to the Atrium or occupied the windows, because a circus was to be exhibited. And at 2:30 P.M. several acts from the Hagenbeck-Wallace circus began. Through a runway built from the ring to the outside of the building came five huge lions and Mr. Schweyer, their trainer. He put the beasts through several stunts with absolute fearlessness, although one of the lions, Brutus, threatened to tear him to pieces several times. The cage was then taken down, and Mrs. Cottrell gave a graceful exhibition of equestrianism with a beautiful big white horse, assisted by a small black pony. Following this came an act by five very large elephants, which performed very intelligently. Concluding the circus performance was a clown and his two boxing dogs, all of which furnished an exciting time for the audience.*
>
> *Salvation army girls then donated doughnuts and boxes of fruit and nuts to the boys, all of which they gladly accepted. The men even ate supper at 5 o'clock. At 7:15 the evening performance began. The Christmas tree and big star were lighted with multi-colored bulbs. The windows were again filled with patients. Entertainment was furnished by the hospital orchestra, a playlet by French Lick people, and professional talent from Indianapolis. The evening was most enjoyable as the afternoon, but the spectators, especially the patients, were becoming fatigued from the constant excitement. Thus passed one of the most unique days that one could possible imagine. Those who have been interested in sending gifts to the patients here at the hospital or in any way contributing to their enjoyment, would sure have had their hearts full of joy at seeing the way the boys appreciated all that was done for them.*

As months passed, and her divorce became final, Lillian could be seen now and again, hand-in-hand, with a Lt. Harold Cooper, one of the recuperating soldiers. Although the armistice was signed with Germany in November, the Hospital stayed in operation until April, 1919 when the 'healed' soldiers shipped out –mostly to their homes across America. And the West Baden Springs Hotel went back to being a hotel again. But things were just not the same anymore. First of all, Lillian planned to set up a meeting with Ed Ballard to discuss the future of the hotel. However, Ballard himself was under great duress from a terrible accident that involved his circus a few months earlier.

THE GREAT TRAIN CRASH

The most horrendous circus train accident in history took place in the middle of the night on June 4, 1918, just outside Hammond Indiana.

One of Ed Ballard's Hagenbeck-Wallace Circus trains filled with up to 400 performers and workers in a long line of sleeping cars was pulling off the main line to switch tracks when behind it barreling along at high speed was an empty troop train on its way to Chicago. It is reported that the engineer on the oncoming troop train had just fallen asleep (according to his later testimony) when his locomotive slammed at full throttle into the rear of the circus train. The long line of wooden sided railway cars crumbled and burst into tremendous flames. The mayhem that followed was a living hell; the enormous collision and resultant explosion caused a scorched earth and wide devastation. Rescue workers who raced to the site had great difficulty dealing with the many who were injured due to the intense heat. By daylight it was a grizzly scene of charred bodies of the dead, many burned beyond recognition. The smoldering ruins were a picture of pure devastation, and the news spread around the world.

Scenes of the impact, 8 am June 22, 1918

On the day of the crash Ed Ballard was not traveling with the circus train in his private railway car as he usually did. Rather he had traveled to Chicago the day before to meet with representatives of the US Tent & Awning Company about purchasing new tents for his circus.

Ballard heard about the terrible accident when he got the message where he was staying at the Congress Hotel in Chicago. He hurried to the scene by automobile and immediately set to work to do what he could to help the situation.

He was devastated to see the tremendous loss of life (86 dead), and the great number of injured (130), many severely. He tended to the needs of the injured, and began making arrangements for the dead. Many of the circus performers and behind-the-scenes workers did not have family nearby or even in America. Ballard always claimed that there was a strong sense of family among the people who worked together in his circus and he saw to it that the injured got the best medical care possible, and for the deceased circus performers and workers, he took care of all funeral expenses, and arranged for burial at Woodlawn Cemetery in Forest Park, Illinois.

Hundreds of mourners attended the services, and the Showman's League of America placed an elephant carved in stone as a memorial at the site that "pays tribute to the men and women who gave so much joy through their performances both in the ring and behind the scenes." Ballard especially mourned for a young man from West Baden he had just hired to join the circus and travel on the road.

The next day in Monroe Wisconsin the signs were hung out: NO PERFORMANCES TODAY. But miraculously, two days later in Beloit Wisconsin, with the help of other circuses around the country, Ballard's circus was able to 'put on a show' to an appreciative, huge crowd. It was solace for the nation, still mourning the terrible loss in "the greatest circus train wreck in history."

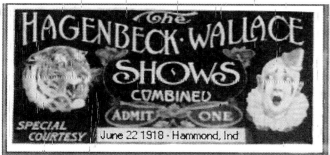

He put the circus up for sale, but within two years, Ballard, with his partners, began the process of putting together a consolidation of many circuses that was to become the largest circus in American history: The American Circus Corporation.

The Post World War I Years

Now with the former army hospital a hotel again in 1919, the difficulties of running the place returned for Lillian Sinclair. She muddled through for a while, but was uncertain about what to do. The new 'Pompeian Court' in the Atrium was still attracting attention, and some new patrons, but soon Prohibition of the sale of alcohol became the law, and new travel habits set in -along with 'speakeasies,' bath tub gin, flappers, vamps, and Ding Dong Daddies.

It was also when Lillian first sat down with Ed Ballard and began negotiations on what to do with the West Baden Springs Hotel. Ballard's reputation at the time was legendary: there were his many holdings in real estate, his several gambling establishments, and now his 'largest traveling circus in the world.'

Also Ballard owned more gambling clubs, and some of the most famous hotels, and real estate from Florida to California. A sampling: he owned the Palm Island Club and the Tea House Plantation in Miami; he had interest in the Nationalle in Havana, a casino in Saratoga Springs, the Kentucky Club in Hot Springs (Arkansas), the Congreve Hotel in Chicago, thousands of acres of beach front property and land in many states. In Springs Valley he owned the Brown Club, the Winter Quarters for his circuses, the Hoosier Club, the Homestead, and the Round Trip Inn. There now was no question that the three names behind the phenomenal success story of Springs Valley were Taggart, Sinclair, and Ballard.

At first, Lillian was hoping that there would be a way to share ownership of the hotel with Ballard. But it was a difficult position for her because her debt to Ballard of the $500,000 borrowed by Charles Rexford. Also, the hotel needed to be renovated from an army hospital back to a hotel, something that Lillian could ill afford. Finally, she agreed to sell the hotel for $1,000,000 which meant that Lillian would receive $500,000 from Ballard, and the $500,000 loan to Rexford would be considered paid up. With this sensible agreement completed, Lillian moved to California with her new husband, Harold Cooper, where they lived out their lives, happily, together.

Ed Ballard is New Owner of West Baden Springs Hotel

Ballard hired a strong team, mainly from other hotels he owned across the country, to help run his West Baden Springs Hotel. (Years earlier with no hospital in Orange County, Ballard's son Chad, after a pony cart accident at the circus winter quarters, had to be taken all the way to Louisville for medical treatment. The delay of treatment caused gangrene to set in, and the boy's leg had to be amputated. So Ballard felt very strongly about having a hospital in Orange County.) He straightaway improved the baths, the dairy, the farms, and set up a well-equipped hospital in the outer rooms of the hotel's sixth floor, and had the spa baths moved to the inner rooms. Dr. C.W. Dowden headed up the talented staff of doctors and nurses. Soon patients came from all around the area, and if they had no money with which to pay, then there was no charge.

Ballard's efforts gave the West Baden Springs Hotel a needed lift. Soon, he brought in big name orchestras and other spectacular entertainment, and the number or rich and famous guests increased: General John Pershing, Governor Al Smith of New York, Mayor Bill Thompson of Chicago, Irving Berlin, Abbott & Costello, Lana Turner, and many other stars of stage and screen again visited the hotel.

By 1924 there was a surge in convention business –for example the National Rotary Club banquet was set up in the shape of a huge wheel, resembling the organization's trade-mark symbol. And more than a thousand dinners were served.

Besides the stage shows in the Atrium, Ballard continued his spectacular circus acts that astonished spectators in the Atrium. By 1929, it looked like Ballard, now one of the richest men in the country, was unstoppable. And that's when it happened.

THE STOCK MARKET CRASH

There was a convention in the Atrium on that fateful day in 1929 when the podium speaker was handed a note from an employee of the on-site stock brokerage firm located just off the lobby. It told the news that the Stock Market had crashed, and Wall Street was spinning out of control.

Within days attendance at the hotel started to decline drastically, and over the next two years, Ballard paid his staff while less and less income was coming in. Soon unemployment began to spread across the country. People looked for answers for an American economy spinning out of control. People lost their homes and were left with no safety net. And the workers at the West Baden Springs Hotel wondered how long the beneficence of Mr. Ballard could hold up with hardly any patrons reserving rooms. But somehow, across town, the French Lick Springs Hotel seemed to be holding its own.

Maybe it was the ubiquitous Pluto water and recent renovations that kept people coming to the French Lick Springs Hotel. The North Wing had been added a few years earlier, which included many new hotel rooms, conference rooms, and a convention hall. Pluto's Well, and the glass domed swimming pool, gardens, etc., were now on the interior side of the hotel, no longer seen from the street, and the new iconic canopy was added over the marble steps, making it the new entrance. With Tom Taggart Jr. now running the day-to-day operations, his father became the symbol of the storied past. (In her libretto for *Show Boat*, Edna Ferber wrote, "In the evening we can take a whirl at Tom Taggart's layout … The last time we were down I won a thousand at roulette alone!" Taggart sued, and the allusions to Taggart were cut out of future renditions of the show.)

PLUTO WATER EVERYWHERE

Pluto Water continued to be shipped around the country in freight car loads. Americans could see the red devil Pluto printed on the sides of boxcars as the trains roared along the tracks through the countryside. Then in drugstores nationwide there was always a shelf stocked with Pluto Water. These displays of the Pluto image continued to be running advertisements for the French Lick Springs Hotel. Taggart's address books had listed the names of salesmen in most of the major cities, even though he admitted that "the waters are not a cure—at all." Pluto Water sales had reached $1,200,000 in 1912, and only grew over the next decade.

In 1922, the capital stock of the French Lick Company was increased from $600,000 to $3,000,000, and shares were spread fairly evenly among Taggart's wife and children. With his son now running the hotel and his health on the decline from 1925 on, Taggart began spending his time out of the spotlight, enjoying grandchildren, and his several behind the scenes political forays.

The high and sometimes low dramas swirling around the often bigger-than-life characters in the saga of the Springs Valley grand hotels in the early days in Springs Valley were endlessly fascinating. But even more remarkable were the luxurious and elegant life styles they built for themselves and their patrons. It was truly the Easy Life.

The Golden Age

When looking back on the sweep of history, from the Gay 90s through the Roaring 20s, when travel became common all across the country, when new forms of luxury made daily living less and less a chore, when the great technological revolution reshaped the country's entertainment and communication industries, we can see America's true Golden Age. It was a long time since there had been a major war, and the standard of living had improved immensely in America. It was as if the best of the Victorian Era had drifted into the 20th Century's modernity, and Springs Valley, in Southern Indiana enjoyed a golden age 'sponsored' by its two magnificent grand hotels.

THE HIGH LIFE

Imagine it is 1925, and a young couple is on their way to building a successful and comfortable life style; they possess a number of things their parents' generation didn't have: a automobile, a refrigerator, electrical power, a phonograph player, a radio, and many 'modern' appliances. They leave their home on the outskirts of Indianapolis for a long weekend. They go to Union Train Station with their suitcases, and take the three hour trip south on the Monon Line down past the fertile farm fields, the rolling hills and villages of Southern Indiana, and arrive at he French Lick train station, surrounded by beautiful beds of flowers. They step from the passenger car just a short walk from the beautiful new entrance to the magnificent French Lick Springs Hotel. They have a lazy dinner, listen to the orchestra on the front lawn bandstand, then retire for the evening.

When they wake up in the morning, what do they have to look forward to? First, check the *Daily Schedule*.

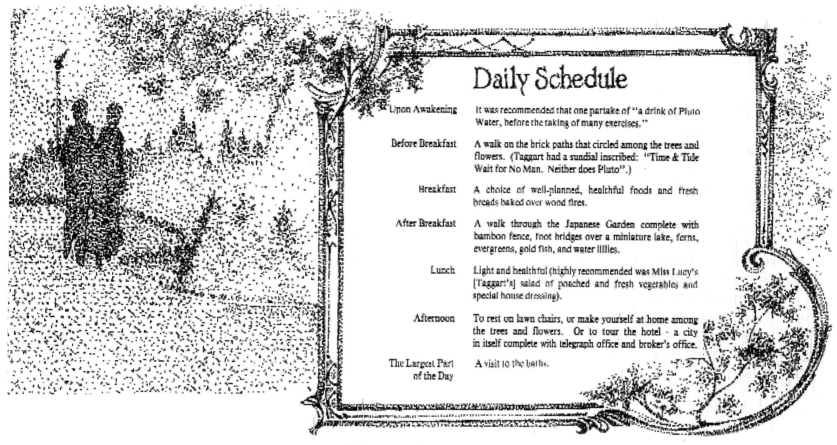

Daily Schedule

Upon Awakening	It was recommended that one partake of "a drink of Pluto Water, before the taking of many exercises."
Before Breakfast	A walk on the brick paths that circled among the trees and flowers. (Taggart had a sundial inscribed: "Time & Tide Wait for No Man. Neither does Pluto".)
Breakfast	A choice of well-planned, healthful foods and fresh breads baked over wood fires.
After Breakfast	A walk through the Japanese Garden complete with bamboo fence, foot bridges over a miniature lake, ferns, evergreens, gold fish, and water lillies.
Lunch	Light and healthful (highly recommended was Miss Lucy's [Taggart's] salad of poached and fresh vegetables and special house dressing).
Afternoon	To rest on lawn chairs, or make yourself at home among the trees and flowers. Or to tour the hotel - a city in itself complete with telegraph office and broker's office.
The Largest Part of the Day	A visit to the baths.

THE BATHS

The baths include: Turkish, Russian, 50-50, Pluto, Oxygen, Nauheim, Vapor, and Cabinet Baths, Salt, Oil, Witch Hazel, Cocoa butter, Talcum and Friction rubs and massages. A special bath elevator serves all floors, and brings hotel guests directly to the baths. One can find bulletins that claim the 'baths' help alleviate "diseases of the stomach, liver, intestines, gall bladder and ducts. Also, auto intoxication, indigestion, rheumatism, diabetes, obesity, malnutrition, the urinary system, skin, nervous system, kidney diseases and arteriosclerosis."

Walking through the hallways, or the grounds, one might see some of the rich and famous visitors who add to the luster of the hotel.

DINNER

Dinner is a feast to behold: food elegantly prepared under the guidance of world famous Chef Louis Perrin is served by waiters with trays atop their heads. The menu features such delicacies as "Barbecued Opossum with Southern Candied Yams, Grilled Tenderloin Steak Creole, Broiled Fresh Mushrooms on Toast, Omelettes, Fritters". (As early as 1912, long before it was comercially packaged, an original concoction, 'tomato juice,' was being served at the hotel.)

AFTER DINNER

The hotel orchestra provides music for dancing in the gorgeous Dance Pavilion. Guests retire from the dining room – men in their tuxedoes, and ladies in all their splendor of evening dresses and jewels, may dance the night away.

AFTER DANCING

The ladies retire to their rooms to begin another day refreshed. Then, many of the gentlemen leave for activity across the street at Brown's, or some other casino. And after some time of taking their chances, they will retire to their rooms. The next morning the young couple will be ready for a day or two more of elegance, and then ride the rails back home, all the way reliving their holiday, and already planning the next one.

WEST BADEN EXPERIENCE

In Chicago, a middle aged wealthy couple, who have been traveling to the West Baden Springs Hotel for years, for seasonal stays, step into the back seat of their roadster for a Spring trip to West Baden. Their driver will follow a planned route of stops for meals and rest at country clubs and well known restaurants along the way. Also, they may stop for an overnight with old friends.

When they reach West Baden in the late morning, they are excited to walk their favorite garden path to Spring Five, while their luggage is set up in their favorite room on the sixth floor with a balcony that looks out onto the magnificent atrium. After their indulgences with the out-of-doors, they will relax in their room, dress for the afternoon, go down to the elegant dining room for lunch with old friends who also are accustomed to seasonal stays at the 'Carlsbad of America.'

After lunch a horseback ride in the rolling hills is followed by a trip to the salon by the ladies, and, by the men, a venture to the baseball diamond to watch a major league baseball team in spring training.

After bathing, and dressing for dinner and drinks, they will hob nob with another set of old friends, during dinner and entertainment, and watch for glimpses of famous movie stars, sports, or business titans, walking among the elegantly dressed crowd. They will later retire to their rooms as they hear --wafting up from below-- the distant strands of violin and piano from the house orchestra's closing music for the evening. And so to sleep, breathing in the soft country air as they complete their first day in their stay at the beautiful West Baden Springs Hotel.

In the days ahead, they will visit the baths, take walks among the special trails that are part of the 'health tonic' they've come for, and after their extended stay, will take their slow journey home to Chicago, planning their next journey back, along the way.

THE LAST YEARS OF A LIFE WELL LIVED

In all his adult life, Tom Taggart could not get enough of politics. During his last term as Mayor of Indianapolis, he began the process of purchasing the French Lick Springs Hotel and he shifted his interest to behind-the-scenes politics where he became a powerhouse. Earlier, he had held court with many political allies in the lobby and restaurant of his own Grand Hotel in Indianapolis. Then, in 1901, with a growing reputation, his interest became 'national' as a member of the Democratic National Committee, and a new owner of the French Lick Springs Hotel. He simultaneously built up his new hotel and became a very successful entrepreneur with interests in various businesses in Indiana and beyond, that included selling his hotel's Pluto Water across the country.

But most of all he became Chairman of the Democratic National Committee, and promoted his own political candidates for the presidency of the United States almost every four years from his perch in his penthouse atop the French Lick Springs Hotel. Always staying close to friends in Indianapolis, Taggart had magnificent houses on Capitol Avenue, then built an estate on Delaware Street in 1914. When his health started to decline in the mid-1920s, he still kept up his political efforts, mainly from his base at the French Lick Springs Hotel, even though he spent stretches of his wintertime with his family in Palm Beach or Miami Florida where he would have sessions with Democratic leaders from across the country.

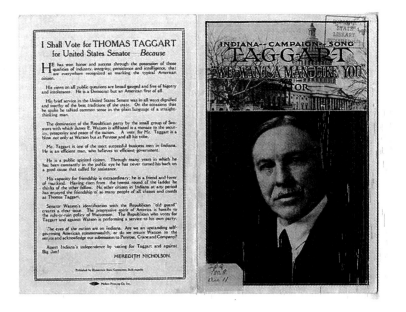

The 1924 election was devastating for Taggart, in that he had a candidate withdraw (Ralston), a hand-picked candidate for governor (McCulloch) lose badly, and the Democratic ticket itself (Davis/Bryan) was devastated in a landslide won by President Calvin Coolidge. Also, Taggart, who had been suffering from severe 'stomach problems' for some time, had major surgery in 1924, after which he went into a slow but definite decline. But he did continue to serve on boards, and became a major partner in a company in Louisiana set up to drill for oil and natural gas –which he was very active in and he visited the site often.

By 1928, with his son fully running French Lick Springs Hotel, Taggart had two missions he wanted to fulfill: one was to build glorious homes for his children, and the other was to make one last effort to promote a Democratic candidate to become president of the United States. He chose Evans Woollen of Indianapolis who was a Yale graduate, a railway attorney, and bank president, to run for national office.

"It will be my last fight. I believe I have one more fight in my system, one last stand, and, by Jove, I'm going to make it." At the Democratic National Convention in Houston, Taggart's doctors forbade him to attend. Sadly for Taggart, at the convention his fellow Democrats chose New Yorker Al Smith who was the first Roman Catholic nominee. Smith would go on to lose in the general election to Herbert Hoover. Alas, Tom Taggart who did get to spend some time as an appointed US senator from Indiana during Woodrow Wilson's administration was to end his storied career of 'king-maker.'

On June 17, 1928, Tom and Eva Taggart celebrated their fiftieth wedding anniversary amidst praise, gifts, and the love of family and friends.

Taggart had earlier provided houses in Hyannis Port for daughters Nora and Emily. Now his concentration was on two more houses for two more children: a beautiful estate for Lucy Taggart on Eastern Point in Massachusetts, and what is commonly called a mansion for Tom Jr. in French Lick.

(Photo of family members at Tom and Eva Taggart's fiftieth wedding anniversary celebration. The guests of honor are seated front and center.)

Kennedy Compound, Hyannis Port
Taggart Compound, Hyannis Port

From Cape Cod to Mount Airie

The elegant home built especially for Tom Taggart Jr. had a heartwarming story behind it. It begins with the remarkable fact that perhaps the two most successful behind-the-scenes democratic operatives of the 20th Century, Thomas Taggart and Joseph P. Kennedy, should be accidental summer neighbors on a Massachusetts shoreline.

In 1915 Thomas Taggart purchased property and built a sprawling mansion called Amyville (after Taggart's ancestral village in Ireland), on the shore in Hyannis Port, on Cape Cod. In 1923, Joseph P. Kennedy purchased property for his own large enclave right next door. Tom Taggart's east-coast summer escape had provided glorious times for the Taggart brood over many years. And generations of Kennedys basking on their sailboats, or playing touch football on the lawn were images that would become part of the American psyche years later as many of the Kennedys became famous politicians.

Joseph P. Kennedy

Thomas Taggart

As it happened the two Irish-American families had their friendships and their disputes: The Kennedys once sued the Taggarts in a quarrel over the placement of a pier and right-of-way on the borderline between their two properties. After a rather bitter dispute, a compromise was worked out, and soon the two families joined in neighborly social events. Because the Kennedy children -Joe, Jack Bobby, Teddy, Kathleen, etc. -were roughly the same ages as the Taggart grandchildren, Kathleen Kennedy dated grandson Thomas Taggart Sinclair (unrelated to the Sinclairs of West Baden Hotel). Sinclair also engaged in spirited wrestling on the front lawn with the future president, Jack Kennedy. On many occasions, they all went to each other's house to watch the latest movies on a $15,000 machine called a vitaphone, which each family owned. And they often sailed together. In short, they lived the good life as close neighbors. Tom Taggart Jr. especially loved his Cape Cod summer home, and his father took note. Meanwhile, back in Indiana, Tom Taggart, despite declining health, purchased a parcel of land with a 100-foot high lookout tower called Mount Airie just outside French Lick, on the highest hill in the area with a magnificent view. He had the tower torn down, and decided it was the perfect spot to build an elegant home for his only son. It was a magnificent brick replica of the Taggart's wooden Cape Cod mansion, and it fit perfectly on that high spot where the rolling hills spread out over a large batch of tree-dotted hills sporting evergreens, maples, tulip trees, ash, and many species of wild flowers.

Sadly, Taggart Senior died before the home was completed in 1929, so he didn't get to see how perfectly it turned out. A drive up an old-winding road leads to that seemingly out-of-place, out-of-time, grand replica that was also called Mount Airie. It is there that Tom Taggart, Jr. and his family lived for years.

The story of Mt. Airie has the makings of a fairy tale. How, once upon a time, a prince in his own fantasy life inherits a fortune, and the attendant power of his famous father's name made in politics, and as owner of the famous French Lick Springs Hotel, the father builds the son a castle that is a replica of where he lived happily as a boy when time stood still. Stately buildings, stables, gardens, guest houses, and many other amenities brought great pleasure to everyday living. But most of all the surrounding display of extraordinary nature at work, gave Mt. Airie a touch of perfect bliss on Earth, a fairy tale come true.

In reality, of course, there was a hotel to keep up in a difficult economy, loyalties to maintain, decisions to make in a rapidly changing world. Tom Taggart Jr., a quiet man, with a warm personality, was respected for his skill in taking his grand hotel through the Depression and war, then selling it off as a valuable property when he retired in 1946, a happy man. But in November 1929, when he moved into his beautiful home for the first time, his thoughts were with his father.

When Thomas Taggart died on March 6, 1929, he was surrounded by family members at his Delaware Street home in Indianapolis. Two days later funeral services were held in both Indianapolis and French Lick.

In Indianapolis, Bishop Joseph M. Francis of the Episcopal diocese read from the *Book of Common Prayer* and offered a eulogy which stated that Taggart lived "with a purpose and a vision. His integrity in public office, his winsome personality endeared him to a great multitude. A valiant fighter and yet a more valiant loser, who harbored no grudges, and bore no malice, he has left a heritage which will endure."

In French Lick there were two services, one for Blacks at the African Methodist Episcopal Church, and one for Whites at the French Lick Methodist Episcopal Church. At two p.m. all businesses, including the hotel in French Lick, closed --allowing hotel employees and townspeople to attend the services.

All over Indiana flags were lowered to half-mast, and at the State House, and at many political gatherings around America, Taggart was fondly remembered for his many contributions to his country over the years.

MUCH KINDNESS AND LITTLE MISUSE OF POWER

Tom Taggart Sr. had made his grand hotel world famous and a national gathering place for the Democratic Party. He will also be remembered as a major force in American politics and hotel-managing in the grand style. Tom Taggart had made his mark on America, and his obituary in *The New York Times* proclaimed:

> *"Mr. Taggart enjoyed every moment of his life, and leaves behind him the memory of much kindness and little misuse of power."*

The hotel's grand lobby captures the elegance of the "Taggart Era."

A postcard for the hotel during Taggart's heyday.

A "typically Taggart" Christmas card sent to friends, business associates, notables and the notorious.

Tom Taggart Jr., who had begun running the day-to-day operations of the hotel years earlier, was now the face of French Lick Springs Hotel, and even spent some years in the 1930s active in Democratic politics. But his main focus was keeping a hotel going during the Great Depression, which he did.

French Lick Springs Hotel waiters provided patrons with efficient, elegant and unique (tomato juice was invented at the hotel) fine dining experiences. Taggart's extensive culinary, housekeeping, grounds keeping, maintenance, spa and transportation staffs not only contributed to the comfort and pleasure of guests, but also to the economic stability of the Valley.

Rich and Famous

Still, the rich and famous, and the powerful came in droves to Taggart's hotel. A guest list circa 1930 (compiled by Richard Haupt, an excellent historian of the hotel's early years) could easily have included:

George Ade, Pauline Fredericks, William F. Kenny, Nicholas F. Brady, R.E. Frest, Frank A. Dudley, Julia Boyd, Gene Tunney, Charles B. Dillingham, Leon Errol, W.A. McGuire, Irving Berlin, Jake Rupert, Mary Roberts Reinhart, the Vanderbilts, M.F. Plant, John W. Gates, Al Smith, Charles F. Murphy, Roger Sullivan, and the list could go on and on. Hundreds of senators, governors, and other politicians visited French Lick at one time or another. The roster of famous names would have read like a Who's Who of the early 20th Century. It was style, it was fashion, to visit French Lick. 'Society' preferred to visit Tom Taggart's resort in Orange County.

The Legacy of Tom Taggart is one of being a great hotelier, a major national political figure, and a quintessential family man. He will also be remembered for putting a permanent stamp on Springs Valley.

AL CAPONE & F.D.R.

In the annals of 20th Century history, the names of two men call to mind a perfect antithesis of good and evil: they are Franklin D. Roosevelt and mobster Al Capone. Both had a part to play in the history of French Lick Springs Hotel and West Baden Springs Hotel. Capone's home town, Chicago, was the principle city feeding people into the French Lick and West Baden hotels. And as the best known mobster in a city known for mobsters, Capone became a public figure and engaged in both social and criminal activities. Bootlegging during prohibition was Capone's principle illegal activity, yet he regularly enjoyed the public spotlight.

Once upon a time, in a chauffeur-driven bullet-proof roadster, Capone traveled to French Lick to get married in one of the elegant houses that stood between the two hotels. Capone's ceremony became a public event; he was treated like a visiting head of state. It was planned that once the ceremony was over, the wedding party would gather for a reception at the French Lick Springs Hotel. But one story has it that Taggart stood firmly at the door, barring it from the Capone party, and he stormed away to go to the other hotel up the way. Another story has it that Capone was first turned away from the West Baden Springs Hotel. The truth is up for grabs.

In 1931, with Tom Taggart, Jr. managing the hotel, what has become a political milestone took place. The National Governor's Conference convened at French Lick Springs Hotel, and among its rostrum was New York's popular Governor Franklin Delano Roosevelt. Meetings were held to establish a Democratic candidate to fight Hoover for the presidency, and the powers-that-be decided to back F.D.R. for the nomination at the upcoming national convention. Eighteen months later, with the victory of Franklin Delano Roosevelt, America elected its longest serving and one of its most heralded Presidents. This was the fourth presidential election greatly influenced in French Lick. The legacy of the Taggart Sr.'s behind-the-scene influence lived on.

THE AMERICAN CIRCUS CORPORATION

The American Circus Corporation was a consolidaton of the Sells-Floto Circus, the Hagenbeck-Wallace Circus, the John Robinson Circus, the Sparks Circus, and the Al C. Barnes Circus. Ed Ballard, who partnered with Jerry Mulligan and Bert Bowers, was principle owner. Among the acts: the emerging great animal trainer, Clyde Beatty, who began with the Hagenbeck-Wallace extravaganza. Among the 50 or more clowns traveling with the circus was the most famous clown of all --Emmett Kelly. And, legend has it, that famous early television star Red Skelton was born on an American Circus Corporation tour. Skelton's father, Ted, was a well-known clown.

Madison Square Garden

Rival businessmen often commented that Ed Ballard's great success was that he had a sure instinct for knowing when to buy and when to sell. For instance, in early 1929, Ballard took over the famous Casino Nationalle in Havana Cuba, and while there he ran into Frank Bruin who headed up the most notable sporting arena in American, New York's Madison Square Garden. The two became friendly right away, and at dinner one evening Bruin explained he had a delicate situation in scheduling, and asked for Ballard's help.

The problem was that each spring Bruin had been leasing out Madison Square Garden to Ballard's circus rival, John Ringling, of the Ringling Bros. Barnum & Bailey Circus. The arrangement for years had been that Ringling would have to break down his circus each Saturday so that sporting events could be held, but Ringling had decided that he didn't want to do the Saturday break down anymore. Bruin invited Ballard to bring his circus to 'the Garden' so long as he'd do the Saturday break down for the sporting event. Ballard agreed, and the new plan was set in motion. When Bruin told Ringling of the new arrangement, he hit the ceiling.

It was a few days before the Stock Market Crash – October 1929, when Ballard received the call from Ringling who said, "You buy me out or I buy you out." Ballard paused a moment, and said, "Make me an offer."

The price accepted was 1.7 million dollars, and Ballard's timing was prophetic again. Ed Ballard's American Circus Corporation and Ringling Brothers, & Barnum & Bailey Circus had been the two biggest competitors in America, so when Ballard's circus was purchased by Ringling he had a virtual monopoly on traveling circuses in America. And Ballard got out just before its major decline began.

Yes, Ed Ballard's business acumen was astonishing. He spent his younger years, and early adulthood becoming a 'self-educated' man. He read voraciously, he pulled himself up by his bootstraps, and he carefully watched how successful business people do what they do. And now, at the apex of his career, he was at the top of the world in a number of undertakings.

The Decline of the Traveling Circus in America

Over the next few decades, the great traveling circuses in America gradually began going out of business year by year. The great trainloads of everything from elephants to grease painted clowns to canvas and poles for huge 3-ring tents literally had the rails pulled out from under them as travel and freight transportation came under the aegis of the automobile, the many wheeled truck, and eventually airfreight. People were moving to the cities, the new 'talkies' were drawing people to movie houses, and many homes now had radios. The traveling circus across America was losing its audience to 'other' distractions.

The decline in attendance at West Baden Springs Hotel continued in 1930, as people began to realize that the Wall Street crash was turning into a sharp economic decline, nationally. But Ballard's loyalty to his West Baden Hotel staff continued. Then one day in the Fall of 1931, not a single person registered for a room. Ballard closed the doors of the hotel deciding to re-open in May of 1932, but by then the whole country was frozen in a Great Depression, and Ballard closed the doors for good on July 1, 1932. On that very day, he also, sadly, closed the Sixth Floor Hospital. An era ended, and people wondered what would now happen to the "Eighth Wonder of the World."

Ballard unsuccessfully searched for a buyer, and other than a few offers from those he considered "unsavory characters," he couldn't find one. And by early 1934, Robert Graham, founder of the Graham-Paige Automobile Company suggested he give the hotel away to the Society of Jesus, a Catholic Order training Jesuit priests. Ballard had given away properties before over the years, so he pulled his family together to help him make a decision. By then the Vatican had given permission for the space to become a seminary, and Ballard's family agreed it would be a good idea.

WEST BADEN SPRINGS HOTEL BECOMES A COLLEGE

So starting in 1934 the West Baden Springs Hotel for the next several decades transitioned into an education institution --the Jesuit 'West Baden' College, a school for young seminarians, concentrating on the study of philosophy and religious history. O'Malley, once a student at West Baden College, describes the transition. The Jesuits had suggested that they wanted to call it Ballard College. But Ballard refused, and suggested West Baden College be the name for the Jesuits' new college.

The Society of Jesus, an educational organization of priests within the Catholic Church, was founded in 1540 by Saint Ignatius Loyola and played an important part in the Catholic Counter reformation. The members of the Society undergo a long period of training according to strict and austere rules. The West Baden Springs Hotel had to be made to conform to the spirit of its new owners, in accordance with the instructions received from the Father General of the Society in Rome –in Latin, no less.

Reverentian vestram enize adhortor ut inde ab initio ab isto aaedificio seculeamoeat non solum omnen speciem luxus, sed insuper ea omnia quae mundum quovis modo sapient, etiamei ad noc efficiendum majjores expensae fieri debent.(I urge your Reverence to remove immediately everything that looks luxurious or that smacks of a worldly spirit, even if it is costly to do so.)   --translated by O'Malley,

Because of this dictum from Rome, the baths and other elements of luxury were soon to be removed, and where possible, the building was to be converted into a Spartan environment.

In accordance with this directive from the Father General, the Jesuits set about transforming the hotel into a house of study and prayer. The inner rooms were stripped of their furnishings and their walls were covered with book shelves. The baths on the upper floor were torn out and converted into small chapels where the priests of the community could offer Mass each day. The grand ballroom was partitioned into two classrooms and a large auditorium. The dining room was dispossessed of its drapery and carpets, and a large pulpit was installed from which Scripture and other religious books could be read to the members of the Society during meals. The lobby was made over into the main chapel, to be used for the daily devotions of the Jesuits. In the center of the Pompeian Court a life-sized figure of the Savior was erected, symbolic of the change which had taken place.

There was unease in the local community over the loss of property taxes from the Ballard days and concern over town revenues. The 'Eighth Wonder of the World' certainly had its wings clipped. But after a slow start, the relationship between 'town and gown' became warmer. The Jesuits invited townspeople to come to their gatherings, such as their annual Christmas party, which included cookies and soft drinks and a stage presentation. Soon this became an annual event.

FRENCH LICK SPRINGS HOTEL MUDDLES THROUGH

Meanwhile, in 1936, the *Reader's Digest* nostalgically listed the mineral spas still holding on: "French Lick; Saratoga; White Sulpher Springs, Virginia; Bedford Springs, Pennsylvania; and Hot Springs Arkansas." Despite their former success, they were all part of a dying species, the article maintained. But those that adjusted to the changing world, such as Hot Springs and French Lick, carried on somewhat better than the others.

As the new President, Franklin D. Roosevelt, was at work on pulling the country out of its most severe depression, and then a world war, the French Lick Springs Hotel, increased its convention business, and held on -even though the Hotel now took on the 'character' of a pleasant country resort, 'off the beaten path.' But by the 1940s, there was a healthy increase in visitors, and the Taggart name still had currency. Tom Taggart Jr. had steered his enterprise successfully through rough waters.

But beneath the great dome in West Baden where the previous lifestyle of luxury was pervasive, a Spartan lifestyle of study, and prayer prevailed.

Thomas D. Taggart

The Murder of Ed Ballard

It could have been the ending of one of the melodramas that toured to the West Baden Springs Hotel's Opera House earlier in the century. But the strange circumstances under which Ed Ballard met his death became a sensational story across America, and spawned many versions. Years later in 1983, in *The Ballards in Indiana*, the 'definitive' version from the viewpoint of Ballard's son Chad, was put forth:

> *Ed began liquidating some of his holdings about 1934 in order to spend more time with his family. He sold or made gifts of his properties in Florida as well as those in and around the Valley. He waived many mortgages or, as in the case of the Riley estate, substantially reduced them.*
>
> *Having toured Europe in 1936, Ed and Dolly stopped in New York for a visit with the children who were attending school in New Haven and Tarrytown before going on to Hot Springs for a visit with his good friend, George Ryan, to whom he had sold the Kentucky Club. They took a suite at the Arlington Hotel. On the evening of November 6, "Silver Bob" Alexander approached Ed, Dolly, and Ryan in a hotel lobby as they left the dining room. After a brief conversation, Ryan and Alexander were invited up to the Ballard's suite and Dolly went into the bathroom to launder some lingerie as was her custom when traveling. Alexander took a chair across from Ryan and Ed who were seated on the sofa. The three discussed the sale of the Palm Island Club which Ed had owned for some time and Alexander claimed he should have shared in the profits of the sale. Ed's explanation that "Silver Bob" shared only in operation of the club and not in ownership of the physical property so incensed the man he drew forth a gun he had carefully concealed and fired at Ed who fell, mortally wounded, breaking the cane upon which he had rested. A second shot rang out and it was thought Alexander had turned the gun on himself. Only later was it learned hat Ryan had intimated to friends he was the killer.*
>
> *Ryan accompanied Dolly to Louisville with the body of her beloved husband. The children were at Madison Square Garden in New York City where Mary was showing her string of prize winning English ponies. Chad had gone to be with her for the show. Told of the tragedy, they left immediately to join their mother in Louisville for the sad journey to West Baden.*

The Indianapolis Star's obituary was one of thousands:

Charles "Ed" Ballard

Charles Edward Ballard, who rose from humble obscurity in Orange County and French Lick Valley, to become world famous as a millionaire sportsman, casino operator, and circus magnate, today was buried in impressive services conducted by the Order of Jesuits, whom he had befriended. The body reposed in a magnificent flower banked casket in the great atrium of the West Baden Springs Hotel, now the concourse of the Jesuits' West Baden College. Ballard had given the noted hostelry and acreage around it -a gift valued at four million dollars to the brotherhood of monks three years ago.

A stone's throw from the scene of the funeral rites is the site of the bowling alley where Ballard began his climb to wealth and fame.

As the pipe organ, in the chapel adjoining the rotunda, began accompaniment to the men's chorus, a solid phalanx of Jesuit students and priests, in clerical black, flanked the bier.

The funeral service was given by Father Donnelly, rector of the College. He read from the scriptures and his brief sermon dwelt on the benevolences of Mr. Ballard.

The funeral cortege moved to Ames Cemetery, four miles north of West Baden, and there with flowers tempering the grimness of the autumn landscape and the feeble November sun the body was placed in the grave. It was a cosmopolitan crowd, which gathered for the service and internment. Mingling with the somberly-clad monks were wealthy friends, men from the "big top" world, and many, who were frankly curiosity seekers, and scores of old acquaintances from "the valley," who recalled that "Ed" had not been changed by his rise to wealth.

And so the saga of Ed Ballard ended. But his part in making Springs Valley what it became was enormous. Old timers speak mostly of his kindness and generosity. And he helped the world realize how gambling was such an important ingredient in the success of the Grand Hotels in Springs Valley. And yet another era came to an end.

Part Three

The Decline & Fall of Two Grand Hotels

On the Home Front

By 1940-41, America was the major supplier for its allies in Europe who were at war. Then with the Pearl Harbor attack December 7, 1941, the country was suddenly sending thousands of troops across two oceans. All around the country there were blackouts and rationing.

People waited for the news of the terrible fighting in Europe, and the Pacific, as they intently listened to the radio. Also across the country a major drive was begun to get people to buy War Bonds to help the wartime cause. In movie houses, at social events, sports events, and almost everywhere in the land, movie stars and other celebrities made the appeals. Sinatra, Hope, Crosby, Abbott and Costello, Judy Garland and many more joined the cause —and among the most successful drives were those made right in French Lick. The hotel became the site of patriotic zeal. Soon the War Bond Drive was the largest 'fund raising' event in American history, and the French Lick Springs Hotel was one of the leading places that bonds were sold by celebrity after celebrity.

Many young men from French Lick and West Baden went to serve their country in battle grounds in far away places. Troops from the Valley were always surprised to hear troops from other parts of the county say they had certainly heard plenty about the grand hotels. And the two things used to describe Springs Valley were 'gambling' and 'Pluto Water.' During the war, attendance at the French Lick Springs Hotel actually picked up slightly, perhaps because the country was coming out of the Depression.

After years of terrible fighting, the war finally came to an end, and returning troops would find an America that was again vastly changed. However, Springs Valley had pretty much stayed the same. But there were new hotels out in the desert sands of the southwest suddenly emerging on the scene. They even had legalized gambling, and people were flocking there to see its bright lights and roulette wheels. It was called Las Vegas!

CLOSING DOWN

Tom Taggart Jr. after stewarding French Lick Springs Hotel through the Depression, and then the war, surprised many when he sold his hotel for $4,000,000 in 1946 to a New York syndicate headed by John B. Cabot. Cabot's group tried to emphasize the old, the nostalgic, to promote the hotel anew. However, the new owners were soon to realize that with few exceptions hotels out in rural areas had become elegant retreats, and most felt the weight of time. Also, with no Taggart to exert his political influence, gambling enterprises in the Valley were suddenly at risk.

Sure enough, just a few months after Tom Taggart, Jr.'s death in January 1949, there was the "Derby Weekend Raid," as it was called. Governor Henry Schriker, a Democrat, who had made an election year campaign pledge to "put a lid on" gambling in French Lick "for good," sent in a large contingent of state police to close down 'illegal gambling.' The timing of the raid on one of the busiest hotel weekends of the year made a bold statement. And with no prominent Taggart left to make the right 'arrangement' with major politicians, the governor's action stuck this time.

Those returning to the hotel from the Kentucky Derby, enjoying their most exciting weekend of the year of horse racing and gambling, were shocked to find Brown's Casino locked and chained. And they realized that this time it was for good. Soon word spread that gamblers would have to look elsewhere, such as to Las Vegas.

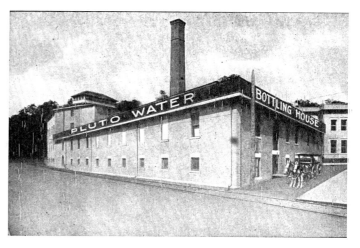

Brown's, which had once attracted high rollers and high society, was torn down a few months later. And the Pluto Bottling Company also was closed down. So the buildings that housed the roll of the dice and the magical waters, the two bedrocks of the Valley, were suddenly gone. It looked like the end had come for the 'Grand Lady,' French Lick Springs Hotel.

New Distractions

By the 1950s young people now had 'other things to do.' Many of those returning from World War II were now attending college in great numbers because of the financial assistance of the new GI Bill, and many were building new homes, and the biggest 'baby boom' of the century was fully under way. Also, many were attracted to the new sleek hotels and hot spots in the swiftly growing urban areas such as Miami, Dallas, Phoenix, Los Angeles, etc. The older generation that had traveled to Springs Valley for generations was dying out.

A family gathers around the living room TV set in the late 1940s or early '50s. (RCA Photo)

By mid century, habits were changing. The love affair with that new thing called 'television' altered how leisure time was spent. Now millions of Americans were staying home and watching Milton Berle's comedy, Ed Sullivan's variety show, game shows, quiz shows, and Edward R. Murrow, who was featured on a new thing called 'the Evening News'. Then by the mid 1950s, the younger generation was suddenly represented on the scene with a new controversial distraction called Rock and Roll music. Some claimed the age of elegance had passed, and a new 'uncultured era' was beginning. This view of a cultural shift was the central theme of Tennessee Williams' popular play, then movie, "A Streetcar Named Desire," where the old elegant lifestyle was replaced by a harsh new reality.

Often the people who came to Springs Valley in the 1950s would nostalgically think back to when they had visited the hotels as children, after arriving on the Monon Railway. Now very few railroad cars chugged into French Lick.

Interstate Highways Replace the Railway

In the Eisenhower years, there was a drive to build new roads, especially new interstate highways, which crisscrossed the land, and, sadly, began to replace the railway. Soon it was impossible to travel to French Lick Springs Hotel by rail. The Monon became a memory.

"Meanwhile at West Baden"

Meanwhile, the West Baden Springs Hotel remained a college in the hands of the Jesuits for almost three decades. But the ongoing expense of keeping the building up became too much for them, and by 1962, they picked up and moved to Chicago. Four years later -1966- another college, Northwood Institute, took over the premises.

Northwood Institute

Northwood Institute (later to become Northwood University) was created in 1959 by two educators -Gary Stauffer and Arthur Turner, when they set up shop in a century old 'mansion' in Alma, Michigan. From the start, their stated mission was to educate "the managers of the future- who would have the skill savvy to become ethically impeccable leaders." They described their institution as "a private, tax exempt, independent co-educational management oriented college actively allied to business and the arts."

One of their first, of many, expansions -with the help of a large gift from private benefactors- was to install an Indiana campus of Northwood at the West Baden Hotel in 1966. They put in place a curriculum that included Restaurant Management, Automotive Marketing, Fashion Merchandizing, Business, Theatre Studies, and Hotel Management -which certainly seemed appropriate, given that they were in what once had been one of America's leading hotels. Over the seventeen years it operated on the West Baden Springs Hotel premises, Northwood Institute educated many students, and became an important part of the community. But by 1983, the old building became too expensive to keep up, and Northwood moved out. As the West Baden Springs Hotel stood empty, all eyes turned to the French Lick Springs Hotel as the last hope for the 'valley.'

Northwood Institute graduates at West Baden in the 1960's

NEW OWNERSHIP FOR FRENCH LICK SPRINGS HOTEL

For nearly all the first half of the 20th Century, a Taggart was in charge of the French Lick Springs Hotel. In the second half of the century, there were several owners. Starting in the mid 1950s it was taken over by a hotel chain, the Sheraton. The Sheraton organization, one of the earliest 'chains,' had a modest origin in 1937 when the partnership of Ernest Henderson and Robert Moore acquired first the Stonehaven Hotel in Springfield, Massachusetts. Henderson and Moore, still without a corporate name for themselves, soon acquired a large hotel in Boston which had a huge lighted sign on its roof "Sheraton Hotel." The young partners decided it was "too expensive to replace," so "Sheraton" became their 'corporate' name. Their hotels became very successful and they purchased many other hotels in a rapid rise on the East coast. They got their big break when "Sheraton" became the first hotel chain to be listed on the New York Stock Exchange (in 1946). And soon the chain was on its way to spreading across the country, then internationally, by adding new and old hotels, and upgrading them. Sheraton took on the grand old French Lick Springs Hotel in 1955. Over the next few years 'improvements' were made:

Six hundred remodeled, air-conditioned rooms, 'modernized' banquet facilities and meeting places were provided for the 'new conventioneer.' The 'renovation' included putting in 'lowered' ceilings, and covering the floors with linoleum, "to help keep heating costs down." Unfortunately, they covered over the decorative cornices above and the marble floors below that made the grand hotel grand. But it might be remembered that 1950s design and architectural styles were not known for revering past classical styles.

The hotel became known as a modern convention center and a steady business flowed to it, and it turned a profit. Then in the 1970s, the Sheraton chain, during another rapid expansion of acquiring leading hotels around the world, and greatly improving the technology of their reservations system, decided to eliminate from their roster all hotels that were more than ten years old. The 130-year-old French Lick Springs Hotel, again, changed hands.

In 1979 a large number of individuals purchased the French Lick Springs Hotel, and under the management of the Cox Organization changed its name to French Lick Springs Golf & Tennis Resort. The hotel now emphasized its outdoor amenities featured at most resorts such as golf, tennis, hiking, horseback riding, and swimming. And a steady stream of conventions continued to come to the hotel. But soon a new real estate concept was brought to the valley.

A New Direction

The new concept was called Time Sharing, a real estate concept which ironically allowed many people to share an escape that once only the rich could afford. Time Sharing, which was becoming popular all over the world, allowed many people to 'own' the same individual 'villa' one-week-at-a-time throughout the year. And in the case of Springs Valley, 'owners' could also enjoy the amenities of the hotel.

The new villas, built on the hotel grounds, with its 2,600 acres of valleys and hills and gorgeous views, were constructed and sold by a company called French Lick Springs Villas, Inc (FLSV). Through a wide advertising sales program, the villas drew people form the major metropolitan areas of Chicago, St. Louis, Indianapolis, Louisville, and Cincinnati and many other areas in the Midwest. The owner of French Lick Springs Villas, Norman R. Rales also purchased the hotel in the mid 1980s from the Cox Organization.

To interest patrons to visit the hotel and then to, hopefully, have them purchase a 'time share unit,' it was decided that an entertainment format that could entice people to come to the hotel was needed. FLSV undertook a search for the entertainment to fit their needs.

Entertainment at the Hotels

Looking back at the hotel over time, it was discovered that entertainment had been a large part of the night activities at both hotels in the early years, especially with Sinclair's Opera House at the West Baden from 1895-1917, and the bands at French Lick Springs Hotel. Musical entertainment at both hotels began on a regular basis in the late 1880s, shortly after a new bandstand was built in front of the French Lick Springs Hotel, where they hired their own orchestra and early evening concerts were held regularly 'on the front lawn.'

By the turn of the century, outdoor concerts became one of the most popular events at the hotel. Patrons of the hotel would gather in front of the bandstand as popular John Philip Sousa music would waft through the summer evening air. By the 1920s, indoor concerts became the rage. It was the beginning of the Jazz Age with bandleaders such as Paul Whiteman, the Dorseys, and many others. These bands featuring famous conductors and artists who arrived by train at the hotel, provided music for listening and dancing to, up through the 1940s. In that era of swing music and jazz, little Springs Valley showcased some of the best in the world. Also, over the years house musicians continued to provide entertainment, principally at holidays, and on special occasions.

After World War II, smaller bands and lounge entertainment filled the bill, as the hotel became less an escape for the rich and famous, and more a getaway for middle class Americans. This became especially true with the new era of the 'villa' guests in the 1980s.

A New Entertainment

In November of 1983, I *[Claude McNeal]* was approached in New York by representatives from the French Lick Springs Villas who wanted to discuss bringing my (American Cabaret) theater company to French Lick, Indiana to do nightly shows in their Convention Hall for an extended run. They felt that these shows that had been running for some time on the East coast, featuring music, dance, multi-media visuals, and an ironic tone, were the kind of entertainment that would work perfectly well in French Lick. After agreeing to go take a look, I was flown, trepidatiously, from New York to French Lick, a town I'd heard of only because of the famous star for the Boston Celtics, Larry Bird.

On the rainy evening we arrived, I saw first, off in the hazy distance, an enormous mysterious looking domed building and was told it was the once famous West Baden Springs Hotel, now closed and shuttered. We then pulled into the entry to the magnificent French Lick Springs Hotel and I immediately became curious about how and why two neighboring grand hotels would have been built there, long, long ago. When I entered into the lobby of the French Lick Springs Hotel that first night, I was amazed at the grandeur, even though the Sheraton 'do over' still covered much of its elegance. Then, when I visited the 'shuttered' West Baden Hotel the next morning, my great curiosity about the grand hotels of Springs Valley made me more fascinated with the idea of the place itself, and as I talked to local people, I began to realize that there was a deep pride in the history. Secondly, I became excited about possibly doing my shows there. I felt our themes about the roller-coaster history of America over time could fit right in with what I was hearing about the two hotels' rollicking history. Shortly, a deal was struck and American Cabaret shows came to Springs Valley. But I wasn't certain how area audiences would respond to "cabaret" shows.

The Story of Cabaret

As Springs Valley hotels had evolved over a century, and more, so had cabaret entertainment, which began as an art form in late 19th Century Paris. "Cabaret" (a 14th Century French word meaning 'wine cellar') became popular in Paris theaters when cabaret performers began challenging the accepted social and political mores of their time through humor, music, and stories. It soon became the most popular form of entertainment in all Paris, and spread throughout Europe in the early 20th Century, culminating in the satirical dramas of Bertolt Brecht –with such works as 'Three Penny Opera' –first produced in Berlin in 1928. Cabaret even spread to Russia, and by the 1960s, around the world. In the 1970s our theater company developed an 'Americanized' form of cabaret that performed in the New York City area. And now it was time to find out if its satiric tone and musical emphasis would fit into the interests of patrons of French Lick Springs Hotel in the mid 1980s. After some theater renovation, and a month of rehearsals, we opened the first show, and lo and behold, American Cabaret shows ignited audiences' enthusiasm and soon were playing to overflow crowds. People came from Chicago, St. Louis, Louisville, Cincinnati, and Indianapolis and were enamored with the shows. We had planned on running the shows in the valley for two to three months, but instead performed there for 3 ½ years, before moving and performing for many years in a larger venue in nearby Indianapolis (eventually performing around the country under the aegis of Claude McNeal Productions.)

Because of our interest in the Springs Valley area, and the grand hotels, my family and I kept our French Lick home and became active in local organizations that benefited Orange County organizations. And we wondered if there might be a way for the West Baden Springs Hotel to b saved, bringing back the extraordinary excitement of long ago.

West Baden Springs Post-College Era

Hope grew in 1985 when Mr. Eugene McDonald purchased the two year vacant West Baden Springs Hotel with plans to "turn it back into the magnificent world-wide destination grand hotel that it once had been in the early 20th Century."

Mr. McDonald had many hopes and dreams of how to do this, and in many conversations we had in his office across from the hotel, he laid them out with a sparkle in his eye. No naysayer could dissuade him. He could look across the street and see, in his mind's eye, the grand old hotel as it once was. He had a constant string of 'potential' investors, some of whom bought into his dream. He shared, step by step, his vision of how, someday, all the elements could be brought together and make the West Baden Hotel grand again. But suitor after suitor faded from the scene. Sadly, the weight of history and time were eating away at the "Eighth Wonder of the World," as it fell deeper into decay.

Then one of his suitors, Marlin Properties of California decided to come aboard: McDonald felt that he finally had found the answer. They worked for some time on a plan which finally got underway. Unfortunately, the deal was structured poorly and dissolved into a legal contest that dragged out and grew worse and worse, finally causing mutual bankruptcies for the partners. People began to feel their high hopes had been dashed.

The "Eighth Wonder of the World" in decline

WHAT DO WE DO?

Now there was new worry in the air. For the people who lived and worked in the valley, it became harder to imagine the return of a glorious past. And they began to wonder what might happen next. As citizens of Springs Valley and Orange County they were from various ethnic and racial backgrounds and it is said that 70% of their forebears were involved directly or indirectly with one or other of the hotels. So, for many, there was a legacy that should be kept up. Old timers remembered hearing with great pride from their previous generations how they built the domed masterpiece in West Baden, or the sprawling yellow brick grand hotel, section by section in French Lick. It was hard to find someone without a fascinating story from the past.

The families who represented generation after generation of kitchen help, waiters staff, maintenance people, housekeeping staffs, groundskeepers, administrative staffs, managers, etc. had put the human touch on the hotels, and it was the human touch that formed the basis of the stories told and retold. They were proud that hotel guests over the years often marveled over the high quality of service from the hotel's staff. Frank Maloney, Manager of the French Lick Springs Hotel for much of the 1980s, remarked that he "had never known a staff so highly praised for their graciousness and real concern by the guests they served." It was not uncommon for returning guests "to ask for this or that employee –as a gesture of fond memories," he added.

Was the impending decline just a bad dream they could wake up from? As the old Chinese proverb goes:

Last night I dreamed I was a butterfly. Today I wonder if I'm a butterfly dreaming I'm a man.

The conversations in restaurants, other public places, and on the street, began to have a more noticeable edge. It seemed that people wanted to start seeing matters as they really were. They were tired of being at the bottom of the barrel in the state economically. And now more and more they wondered what they themselves could do to help save their community, and give it a future.

It became common to overhear phrases that set the mood for a variety of emotions:

"I can't look at it [West Baden Springs Hotel] when I drive by. It's too sad."

"We need another Sinclair."

"The outside world's not going to help."

"What we have to do is start the ball rolling first."

"Mineral water and gambling made this town –they're gone."

"We were the old Las Vegas and Atlantic City, those should be models!"

"I don't see any hope, anymore."

"You have to have hope."

"We need a miracle."

"We need two miracles, one for each hotel!"

"We gotta pick ourselves up by the bootstraps."

But the most common sentiment was: "we need a miracle." But where could a miracle come from?

Hitting Bottom
The Auction Block and Bankruptcy

By the early 1990s, America was at war in the Persian Gulf, and a recession had set in across the land. In Springs Valley, the French Lick Springs Hotel was put on the auction block, and the West Baden Springs Hotel was under the control of a bankruptcy court. The Valley itself had hit rock bottom. The population was on the decline with many of the young leaving, and the old marking time. One way or another, it was perhaps the most ominous moment in time in the history of Springs Valley.

Walking through the West Baden –treacherously—the once fabled spaces lay in ruins: the grand dining salon, once the vibrant host to chattering, elegantly dressed early 20th Century diners looked as though it had sunk with the Titanic in 1911 (absent the deep sea water and curious fish).

The men's card parlor, once the gentlemanly gathering place for boisterous conversation and relaxation looked like Dracula's basement, long after the castle had closed its gates. The grand lobby, once the inviting and glamorous spacious room for people excitedly entering from the classic front steps, now looked so dreary that it was hard to imagine it ever coming back to life.

Outside, the Spring houses such as Apollo, and Hygeia, which once had lines of patrons waiting to partake of their magical powers, now looked like uncared-for Greek ruins, once altars to various gods. And the sunken gardens, once the glory of the nature-loving patrons from far and wide who treasured the up-to-the-minute meticulous grounds keeping, now looked like a long abandoned field, in the process of being reclaimed by nature.

At French Lick Springs Resort, operating at 30%, some of the buildings were still un-air-conditioned, the fabled glass domed pool looked as though it definitely had seen its better days, the lobby had been reconfigured enough times so that it made no architectural sense, the roof had leaking here and then there, the basement had seasonal flooding, and the hearty conventioneers who still brought their groups to the hotel for nostalgic reasons, had to adjust to spaces that hadn't been improved upon for decades.

Now help was immediately needed. If only there were a magic wand to wave and revive the hotels.

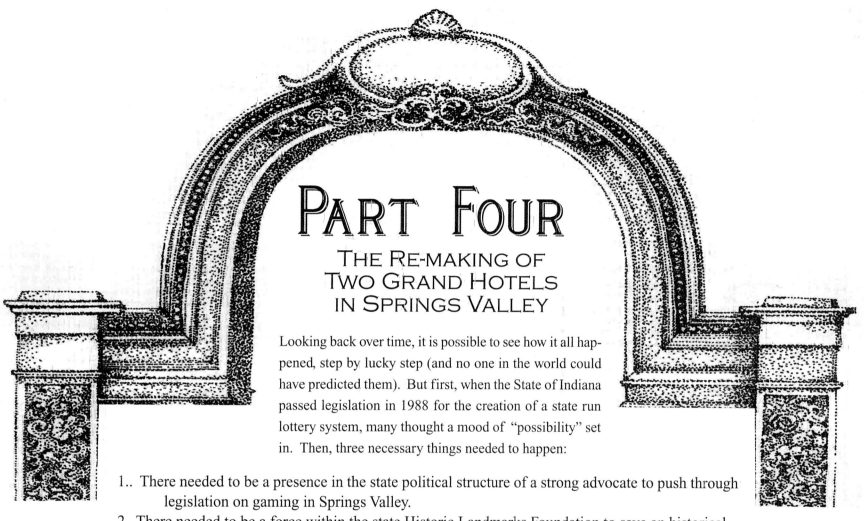

Part Four
The Re-making of Two Grand Hotels in Springs Valley

Looking back over time, it is possible to see how it all happened, step by lucky step (and no one in the world could have predicted them). But first, when the State of Indiana passed legislation in 1988 for the creation of a state run lottery system, many thought a mood of "possibility" set in. Then, three necessary things needed to happen:

1.. There needed to be a presence in the state political structure of a strong advocate to push through legislation on gaming in Springs Valley.
2. There needed to be a force within the state Historic Landmarks Foundation to save an historical building from collapse.
3. There needed to be a philanthropist(s) with a deep love for, and knowledge of, restoration itself. And the means and dedication to pull it all together.

In short there needed to be a few passionate people to become an improbable team acting separately, but ultimately together to bring a future to the community, to save the vital buildings of the past, and even improve the human condition in the process. There needed to be a perfect storm.

Sliver of Hope

Most people at the time didn't know how important a day November 8, 1988 would turn out to be. Following a trend across the country, the voters of Indiana were going to the polls to vote on a referendum to consider a state lottery system. There were strong feelings on both sides of the issue.

Then when the vote count was announced that 66% of the voters approved, some in Springs Valley saw it as a sign of hope. Could this new more favorable attitude toward gambling help save French Lick Springs Resort, and bring back to life West Baden Springs Hotel, and rejuvenate Springs Valley?

With gambling on their minds in Springs Valley, more people began to retell the old stories of how, in the early days, gentlemen visitors to the hotels with a gambling urge had only to go a short distance to Brown's or some of the other local gambling establishments. There were stories handed down about the old gambling establishments that numbered up to more than a dozen at various times. Many told how a five dollar bill pressed in the palm, by a hotel patron, would be followed by directions to the Elite Café, the Club Chateau, the Dead Rat Club, the Babylon Club, etc.

Also, they knew that under the right circumstances, that locals, who were not welcome at most of the gambling establishments, would be welcome at the Kentucky Club, or the Indiana Club. They also remembered with regret how gamblers had taken it as their D-Day when Governor Henry Schrieker made good on his campaign promise back in 1949 to "put a lid" on French Lick gambling once and for all. Now, they wondered aloud if legalized gambling could be the answer to saving the hotels someday.

A Most Important Conversation

A most important conversation took place at the French Lick Springs Hotel in the late 1980s. While attending a convention at the hotel, noted Indianapolis businessman and Democratic activist Larry A. Conrad, talking with local businessman Jerry Denbo, and banker Everett Land, contended that "if legalized gambling were to be the answer to revitalize the Valley, local people needed to be in the forefront of the effort." Conrad challenged Denbo to run for the State House of Representatives so that he could put himself into a position to do something about saving both old hotels through bringing back gambling as the staple that would attract patrons to the valley. Denbo replied, "With such a huge Republican majority in this district, you'd have to be a nut to run." Conrad replied, "Be that nut." Denbo, at great financial sacrifice, decided to do it.

Larry Conrad

Jerry Denbo

The Race Is On

It must be realized that House District 62, which included all or part of five Southern Indiana counties -Orange, Washington, Lawrence, Martin and Green-- had been in Republican hands for years (64% Republican, 36% Democratic, at the time). But Denbo dug in and went door to door, throughout the district, non stop, month after month. As the underdog, he knew it was an uphill battle. But his geniality won him many supporters across the board, and the race tightened.

Then, on election night, to the shock of everyone, Denbo missed winning by less than one percentage point, 50% to 49.9%. It was considered by politicians throughout the state to have been an excellent campaign, and brought great hope for Denbo's future.

Immediately Denbo went back to work for the next election cycle. But this time the Republicans were ready for a fight. Again, Denbo, now better known, went door to door, in this heavily Republican district. Everyone knew it would be a tight election. Finally, after a long campaign, it was cross-your-fingers 1990 election day. People of District 62 voted for a new State Representative, Jerry Denbo!

Denbo's immediately stated goal to the other state legislators was to "save the two historic hotels in Springs Valley." A major persuasion point pushed by Denbo was the well known fact that Orange County had the highest unemployment rate, and was considered the poorest county in the state. And soon the saving of two hotels was a goal that legislators began to call 'Denbo's vision'. Then he dug in, created relationships, and in his first year was able to help pass a house bill in favor of gaming. The House legislation had designated that the two hotels and the short stretch between them as the only place that casino gambling would be permitted.

The House victory stunned many back in Orange County, and further raised hopes. But, sadly, the bill died in the Indiana State Senate. Denbo realized that he had a hard struggle ahead, but he was not about to give up. First, Democrat Mike Phillips was elected the new House Speaker, and he promised Denbo that he would work hard to get his legislation "through the house." This was the beginning of a support system that helped Denbo keep the process going.

No Way But Up

Meanwhile, Denbo, by his persistence brought the story of the hotels to the people around the state. He was the voice in the capitol that brought, first hand, the message of what was happening now in Springs Valley. He reported how the West Baden Hotel had gone empty for many years, and was looking more fragile by the day. Trees and shrubs formed over-growth that seemed to be encroaching on the hotel itself, water seemed to be flowing in wrong places, and causing a real danger of collapse. He also explained that in 1987, West Baden Springs Hotel was listed as a national historic landmark, and was destined to be the most important landmark in the county in need of preservation. By 1989, it had to close its doors even to visitors.

Also, the French Lick Springs Hotel began looking a bit scruffy. The grounds didn't look as meticulous as they used to, and the talk of the town was that it had been up for sale for some time. It became an open question as to whether Springs Valley could, for the first time in a century and a half, end up with no hotel at all. He spread the news throughout the state that he needed help to save Springs Valley.

LUTHER JAMES PURCHASES FRENCH LICK SPRINGS HOTEL.

A small sign of hope was when the French Lick Springs Resort was purchased by Luther James and people breathed a sigh of relief. James, a soft spoken determined businessman who had acquired several hotels in the Louisville area in the past, decided to take on the grand old hotel, which he was able to purchase at auction, in 1991, it was said, for a very low price. He moved into the hotel with his family and immediately had a plan for improvements. In several conversations, Mr. James spoke passionately about what he wanted to do with the hotel. He especially emphasized to me that he wanted to renovate the hotel with a goal of preserving its past glory. He said he felt that people coming to the hotel wanted to experience its history, "to be a part of its glorious past." This meant he would need to undo certain of the Sheraton renovations, and in his first refurbishment phase, he 'unmade' makeovers done during the Sheraton days. But there was a lot to do.

While Mr. James was a diligent leader of the hotel, and did have the means to improve the rather fragile condition of the nearly century old structure, it became more and more clear that some kind of miracle on a larger scale was needed to make good sense out of these legendary buildings looming in Springs Valley, the place of dreams-yet-unfulfilled in Orange County, Indiana. (After a few years, it would come to pass that Mr. James, who had done well by the hotel, sold it to a syndicate from Cleveland, Ohio, the Boykin Group, which maintained ownership for a few years in a declining market.)

Luther James

HISTORIC LANDMARKS TO THE RESCUE

HISTORIC LANDMARKS FOUNDATION OF INDIANA

To make matters worse, there was an emergency at the West Baden Springs Hotel in 1991. An upper outside wall collapsed in the closed up building. (A later study showed that water infiltration caused a structural failure at the roof level which caused the wall to collapse.) The Historical Society of West Baden and others called for the help of Historic Landmarks of Indiana, the statewide organization for preserving irreplaceable old buildings. It was founded by the pharmaceutical Lilly family of Indianapolis in 1960.

Over the years, Historic Landmarks (as of 2010 renamed Indiana Landmarks Foundation) gained national recognition for its aid in saving a number of at-risk important structures. But they had never taken on a project anywhere near as large as the West Baden Hotel. Here was a difficult circumstance: who in the world could help save a closed-up hotel out in the boondocks that some predicted could cost over $100,000,000 to restore. Many wondered if it was worth it to put a 'thumb in the dyke,' because of the enormity of the challenge to ultimately save the whole structure. Was it too late?

Sometimes things dove-tail in mysterious ways. In my days of commuting (1987-94) from our family's home in French Lick to Indianapolis to establish a new theatre, I began a collaboration with J. Reid Williamson, then Executive Director of Historic Landmarks, who was helping me save an historic century-old building in Indianapolis, the Athenaeum, where I was relocating my American Cabaret Theatre. During this time Reid and I often had conversations about the fate of the magnificent old hotel in West Baden. I explained that I thought it was extraordinary, but worried about how it could ever be saved.

Although nowhere near as large as the West Baden Hotel, the Athenaeum, built in 1895 under architect Bernard Vonnegut (the grandfather of novelist Kurt Vonnegut), was also an Indiana treasure. Williamson mentioned that he was extraordinarily interested in, and concerned about West Baden's fabled hotel, especially now because of the collapse of the upper outside wall. He explained how he was talking to people from the West Baden Historical Society, and simply stated, "That landmark just has to be saved." Meanwhile because Williamson and the Historic Landmarks staunchly stood by our efforts in getting the theater started up and rolling along successfully –complete with an historical advisory board that he helped staff— I began to think that with Williamson's passion and commitment, something good just might also happen with the West Baden Hotel.

First, Historic Landmarks supplied the $140,000 from an emergency fund to help toward repairing the collapsed wall. It was a move that kept the dream alive –that thumb in the dyke. Also, Denbo brought fellow legislators to West Baden to see what was going on, which gave his efforts a momentum boost. There was movement. There was hope.

THE KEY DEFINING MOMENT

But a real turning point came when Williamson decided to approach Bill Cook and his wife Gayle for help. The Cooks were known for their preservation work on a number of projects over the years, notably their remarkable restoration of the Colonel William James House (which has an historical connection to the young Abe Lincoln). Also they restored the 1837 'Cedar Farm' (which has become their frequent escape and which includes the main house, work house, milk house, ice house, school house, tenant homes, livestock and tobacco barns –and 2,500 acres of land). The Cooks agreed to meet with Williamson.

Bill Cook

In Bob Hammel's excellent book *The Bill Cook Story* (2008), he reconstructs the scene where Reid Williamson visits Bill and Gayle Cook in Bloomington, asking for help to stabilize the hotel. With great trepidation, Williamson asked for a million dollars. To his great surprise, Cook said yes, then a few minutes later made it two million! It concluded with the famous Bill Cook hand-shake which means that an agreement has been made. This became the key defining moment on the road to the hotel's possible restoration. But there was a mountain of work ahead!

Meanwhile, in 1994, ownership of the West Baden Springs Hotel changed again. Minnesota Investment Partners bought the hotel –with funds from Grand Casinos, Inc. They undertook their project with great enthusiasm, hoping to bring legalized gambling to the valley. But their hopes of creating a casino in the valley were finally dashed when a Denbo gaming bill hit one of its snags in the legislative process. So Grand Casinos put the hotel up for sale for $800,000.

Also during this time, Denbo stubbornly pushed for another gaming bill. The House version called for (1) a land based casino in Gary, and (2) a land based casino between the French Lick Springs Hotel and the West Baden Springs Hotel. (Five riverboat casinos on Lake Michigan and five down south on the Ohio River had won approval a year earlier in the House). Lo and behold, the State Senate voted favorably for five riverboats on Lake Michigan and five riverboats on the Ohio, but changed the French Lick/West Baden Casino plan to nearby Patoka Lake (7 miles away). While this was not exactly what Denbo wanted, it brought the possibility of saving the grand hotels within reach –again. "I kept my foot in the door," he said. So Denbo supported it, even though he didn't fully get what he was striving for. (Little did anyone know that before long, the Army Corp of engineers would determine that no casino could be placed on Patoka Lake.) So if ten of the eleven casino destinations were acceptable, now what? Well, fortunately, Denbo felt that the French Lick option was still alive. And he doggedly fought on.

1994 was the year of the Newt Gingrich Republican surge nationally, and locally, in Indiana, the Democratic majority of 52-48, suddenly reversed to a 57-43 Republican majority. That put Denbo in a tough spot. But in 1995, Denbo introduced a bill to get the Patoka Lake License transferred to the hotel district in French Lick and West Baden. Although Denbo had the ear, and often the support of both Republicans and Democrats, he wondered if he could even get a hearing. And to the surprise of everyone, the new Speaker, Paul Mannweiler, decided to give the bill a hearing. Denbo passionately argued his case in committee. And the bill passed, in committee, eleven to one. This surprising accomplishment drew the attention of the State House, and with it, many opponents of the bill.

When the bill reached the floor of the House, it passed with 66 yea votes. It was a major victory! And there was great hope. However, the senate leader refused to give the bill a hearing, and it died in the Senate. Many Republicans and Democrats were very angry that the bill was not given a chance. And the political drama was now the talk of the whole state. Everyone knew that Denbo was not about to give up.

Another Major Turning Point

Back In West Baden, the Historic Landmarks itself bought the hotel in 1996 for $250,000. This helped cause the major turning point when Bill Cook decided to restore the West Baden Springs Hotel up to the point that it could be put up for sale. "I felt like crying every time I drove by the West Baden Springs Hotel, and knowing it was near collapse, but now with Bill Cook's commitment to fixing it up, it was also a wonderful moment in time and it made me see more clearly than ever, that I had to get the casino bill passed!" said Denbo.

So the monumental task of 'fixing up' the "Eighth Wonder of the World" began. It was what long time Cook architect George Ridgeway called "a rescue attempt." But who knew it was really the beginning of a long journey that would turn out to be one of the major efforts in hotel renovation in American history.

Soon the real work began. Long time Cook associate Joe Pritchett recalls: "In 1996, I was there the first day. Part of the building was coming down, trees overgrown. It was a race to keep it up. We tore all those old walls out and then did all the shoring." Once the building was fully waterproofed, and the existing walls braced against collapse, and the drainage system under the atrium floor repaired and restructured, all the floors were supported with the new steel framing that cut the span of each slot in half. When the slot was still deficient, it was shored in place with metal decking from below. All steel beams were supported by using epoxy anchors embedded into the brick masonry bearing walls. In the dining rooms and ballroom, a new steel framed floor above the original floor had to be constructed, and because one of the walls was "moving away from the building," a new reinforced concrete masonry unit wall was needed.

They also had to rid the old building of truckloads of asbestos, and found out that the fabled concrete construction from 1902 had been deficient, which was why new support, a plethora of new steel beams had to be added. While difficult and time consuming, this fix was an absolute necessity for the huge building, which, after all, was bearing the weight of time and one of the largest free standing domes in the world.

The Process

The work to bring the building up to snuff grew in scope and complexity, and instead of months it would take years, tens of millions of dollars, and loving hands doing intricate restoration. But when it was finished people from the area would be ecstatic and proud to see a remade, astonishingly beautiful hotel. As the restoration started to take shape, the curious came from miles around to gaze upon the operation with wonder. Then the highlight of the 'first phase' was announced: the four 20 foot towers (finials), painstakingly careful reproductions of the originals, would be hoisted in the air by a huge helicopter and gently lowered to their place atop the hotel. This was the most hopeful and cheerful day in Springs Valley in decades:

"I think we surprised ourselves," Gayle Cook told Hammel. "We were all saying, 'Oh, let's do it.' We all knew it was worth saving." "It was on the National Trust's List of Eleven Most Endangered Historic Properties in the United States," George Ridgeway added. "Once we completed the first phase, the project was for sale." Joe Pritchett, whose family had headed up many building projects over the years for Cook, said, "When Bill started in 1996, he was just shoring it up and cleaning it up. It was supposed to be about an eight or twelve month project, and we were there two and a half years." The wonder of it all is that the Cooks just kept the project going.

A Breathtaking Day

It was a sunny October 24, 1998, and *Life Magazine* was there to photograph the event. Five hundred VIP seats at $50 each, and 1,200 standing room seats at $25 each, raised a quick $32,000 for the not-for-profit Historic Landmarks Foundation, which Mr. Cook now supported in a major way.

The exciting event was "the biggest thrill," as Joe Pritchett called it. "I was on the roof for a couple of the towers, and so was Cook, for all four." The 22,000 pound helicopter, flown by Max Evans of Erickson Air Crane Company, was carefully balancing each 19,000 pound tower at the end of a huge holding device hooked to the helicopter. But suddenly the occasion took on the look of an action movie. A 70-mile-per-hour wind draft blew down from the helicopter to the ground, creating the conditions of a small hurricane, and the noise was nearly deafening. People held their breaths. But miraculously, each tower, amidst the loud roar and turbulence, was masterfully slipped into place. There was great cheering.

Meanwhile, Back at the State Capitol

"It was four years during which my casino bill was not given a hearing," said Denbo. "There was an amendment put together to move the license from Patoka Lake. During this time, because of Speaker John Gregg's opposition, no other gambling legislation was voted upon." But it was a victory, of sorts, for the Denbo camp, that the bill to move the license from Patoka Lake (a few short miles from French Lick), was defeated. It was back on the table. Also, Denbo gained respect from the State House for being bold enough to challenge the speaker. The drama continued.

The Competition

Another developing problem by 1999, at the time that French Lick Springs Hotel was changing hands from Luther James to the Boykin Group, was that the new gaming facilities in northern Indiana on Lake Michigan and in the south on the Ohio River were seriously drawing patrons away from French Lick. The Sales Manager at French Lick Springs Hotel said, "From working in the sales office the past ten years, I've continued to see our occupancy go down because of the ten casino properties located elsewhere in the state." As a matter of fact, the Indiana Gaming Commission claimed that these facilities had brought in more than $100 million to the state in wagering and admission taxes alone, in just the first nine months of 1999. It was now more important than ever to get the 'Valley' back into the thick of things. And with the excitement of the beautiful looking West Baden Springs Hotel standing there majestically, many local people decided it was time to help get things moving in the capital. And did they ever. They formed a local group called the Orange Shirts.

THE ORANGE SHIRTS

"It certainly got a lot of attention, and it was a grass roots moment ," said Representative Denbo. A group of avid supporters of Denbo's efforts, dressed in orange shirts and handing out candy and oranges, could be found walking the halls of the State House, pushing for the Orange County Gambling Agenda. Led by Valley resident Jack Carnes, who had supported Denbo's cause from the start, the orange shirts were a citizens' lobby who in the greatest tradition in American politics, constantly reminded the legislators of the need for a gaming bill. Carnes often strategized with Denbo, and kept the Orange Shirts growing in number and enthusiasm. Also, Jim Mathers of nearby Orleans, a Republican county commissioner, offered key support and is considered by Denbo one of his most important supporters in Orange County. He often traveled to Indianapolis as an Orange Shirt, and was roundly criticized by Republicans for "working with a Democrat." The Orange Shirts grew in number and enthusiasm, and were ready to fight to the finish.

Then a turning point in the ongoing legislative battle came when Speaker Gregg allowed a 'loaded' public gambling bill to be heard - and it was shot down! The result was that Denbo gained support for his persistence, and the public began to turn in his favor.

In 2002, three different issues were on the table:
1) dockside gambling for the existing riverboats
2) slot machines at the racetracks, and
3) the French Lick Casino.

There was a huge push by the gaming industry and their supportive legislators for dockside, and the Denbo casino legislation almost made it through, but got defeated at the last minute, some say because of political maneuvering. But most importantly, the public and state House support reached "an all time high." And simultaneously, the Cooks were getting even more involved in the restoration.

Mr. Cook Speaks

Bill Cook summarized: "That building was a wreck. We stabilized it. And nobody wanted to buy it. It was scary." But the Cooks continued, to the delight of all, the incredible restoration work. There was joy in the valley! But now to what use could a renovated building be put?

The Cooks agreed that a building's use is extraordinarily important. Gayle Cook had said, "Finding a use is the key to saving architecture." Suggestions were put forth that West Baden Springs Hotel should become a performing arts center, a health retreat, a religious retreat. Some seemed ridiculous, and none seemed viable. There was no easy answer for the space's use.

The Remark That Changed the World

And then there was the October 2000 event where Bill Cook was making some remarks after being presented with the Outstanding Hoosier Preservation Award-

> *"Gayle and I have run the gamut of the usage of the West Baden Springs Hotel and about the only use we can find would be as an adjunct to gambling."*

This was the moment that made Denbo's job easier. The big puzzle pieces were fitting together. And State legislators took notice. "Bill Cook, for the first time, personally, said the G-word," claims Hammel. And as word spread around the state that Mr. Cook was thinking in terms of gambling, a new defining moment in the journey to the remaking of the two grand hotels was taking place.

The word continued to spread like wild fire in newspapers and by word of mouth. But Bill Cook said of his wife's opinion on gambling, "It was kind of distasteful to her." But, he added, "We were both just enamored with making this thing work." Gayle Cook explained, "I accept the fact that I'm different … you look at all those people having so much fun … I'm not like that, but I accept it." Bill Cook's sentiment on the subject had the sterling clarity that has marked his career as one of America's great success stories. Cook added, "Gaming was never a moral issue with me. The moral issue was to save the hotel. It could have been done as a donation or a gift, but I never like to do any kind of building and not have a prospect of making a profit. Just having a living history is not good enough. The building should be alive and doing its thing. You can't make every building a museum." Now the project had a 'philosophy' to work with. And the leadership of the Cook family guiding it on into the future.

Already, in 2001, Riverboat casino earnings in Indiana would reach 1.84 billion dollars. What if Springs Valley had a riverboat casino? Now, more than ever, Denbo knew he had to get the legislative job done! And he brought more people to see the great progress in West Baden.

Denbo's Magical Year

Speaker Pat Bauer

In 2003 Democrat Pat Bauer of South Bend was elected Speaker, replacing Gregg. Because Denbo's persistence had by now caught the fancy of both the public and both sides in the state legislature, there was a new mood in the legislature and in the state of Indiana. Denbo's House Bill 1902 (the year West Baden Springs Hotel became 'grand') drew more attention and interest than even the state budget bill. There even arose a ground swell of understanding about the need of gaming to save French Lick and West Baden. It was coming to be known that 'Jerry Denbo's vision' -of bringing gaming to Orange County- was getting closer. The "Orange Shirts" crowding the state house halls continued to draw public attention on a daily basis, and those opposing the bill and trying to block legislation, became the target of a great deal of the public's ire.
A new day had dawned!

Representative Jerry Denbo

Victory AT LAST!

It was one of the great moments in Indiana legislative history: The house passed the French Lick Gaming Bill by an overwhelming 84-13 vote, and the senate soon followed by passing the bill 32-20.

And when the results were announced, for the first time in memory a state legislator, Rep. Jerry Denbo, was greeted with a standing ovation when Speaker Bauer summoned him to the Rostrum, and declared: "You have done something that has never been done in history … you have transformed a whole community." It was at that moment that the dedication and tenacity of Jerry Denbo, and the extraordinary vision and leadership of Bill Cook, met at the pass.

House Bill 1902

House Bill 1902 was soon to become the law, and end the thirteen-year odyssey of Representative Jerry Denbo. According to a 'digest' of the Bill 1902:

> The law will establish by ordinance an historic hotel preservation commission with the authority to administer a community trust fund using a portion of the revenues generated by the "riverboat" [casino].

Cook congratulated Denbo, and Denbo praised Cook to the skies. And they both understood how important Historic Landmarks had been in the process.

One Last Step

But there was one more major hurdle --a referendum for the Orange County voters to accept gambling for Springs Valley. There were opinions on both sides of the issue, and it was by no means an open and shut case. "You don't spend twelve years working for something and leave it to chance on the last lap," said Barry Wininger of the Get-Out-The-Vote Effort. A small army of volunteers monitored the polling at the county's twenty two precincts, and Robert Hoyt, Leader of the Orange County Coalition against Legalized Gambling monitored election returns at the county courthouse. While Denbo and others held their breath the votes were counted. With 66% of the voters in favor it passed with flying colors. The last step was over. And it looked like smooth sailing.

So now French Lick was free to have its own casino, legally, for the first time since 1851. But now a new contest was about to begin: who would be the Gaming Commission pick to run the casino?

The Drama Continues

By September 19, 2003, which had been established as the deadline, five entities had put in applications to the Gaming Commission for the right to operate a casino in Orange County: Bally's French Lick, Inc., Jacob's Entertainment, Inc., Orange County Development, LLC., Tranchant Indiana LLC, Trump Indiana Casino Management LLC.

Each group was required to put up a non-refundable $50,000 application fee. The celebrity quotient of the groups was the involvement of French Lick favorite son, former basketball star Larry Bird, of the Orange County Development LLC, and the Donald Trump entity which was already operating in Northern Indiana. There was a good deal of drama in the back-and-forth struggle for favorable position among the various entities in competition.

In July 2004 the commission awarded Trump Indiana the operating contract to construct "a riverboat-style facility in French Lick Indiana." But as Trump and the Commission began negotiating the final terms of the contract, disagreement set in and Trump withdrew from the project and filed for bankruptcy. Now what?

The commission issued a New Request for Proposals on April 6, 2005. The only response was from a new entity, Blue Sky Casino, LLC. The commission reported, "Blue Sky is a joint venture owned by Lauth Resorts & Casino, LLC, an affiliate of Lauth Groups, Inc., an Indianapolis based real estate developer and Orange County Holdings, Inc., a not-for-profit organization formed by the Cook Group of Bloomington, Indiana." Blue Sky was instructed by the commission to present its project by June 23, 2005, when it would be voted upon. Meanwhile, a public meeting was held on April 12, 2005 during which Cook Group's chairman Steve Ferguson stated: "Our vision is to develop the Midwest's finest destination resort, casino, and conference facilty by bringing together two of the most significant grand hotels in the Midwest ... we have been involved for eight years [to] make the vision a reality." On April 13, 2005 the Cook-Lauth Groups purchased the French Lick Springs Hotel.

Blue Sky

Soon after, Blue Sky was awarded an operating agents' contract by the Indiana Gaming Commission to undertake the major transformation of the Valley with both hotels and a casino. Now it was full steam ahead -at last - for the re-making of Springs Valley. First, major work was begun, or continued, on all fronts on both hotels, the casino, and the grounds. The standard had been set with the brilliant level of restoration almost finished at West Baden Springs Hotel. Cook declared that "just an astonishing, beautiful hotel wasn't enough, considering the remote location." That meant upping the ante with French Lick Springs Hotel by giving it the same expansive preservation and luxury upgrade as that at West Baden. Also, there needed to be first class restaurants, swimming pools, spas, shops, to go with the magnificently groomed and historic gardens and grounds at both places. And there needed to be a first class casino –which by state law had to be on the water! Also, the restoration of the famous *Donald Ross Hill Course*, and the creation of the spectacular new *Pete Dye Course* to target avid golfers. The grand scheme of things seemed to be fully on track.

However, there were major 'vision' differences between the Cook Group and the Lauth Group. Cook's insistence on the highest level of materials and workmanship was well known, and Lauth stressed an emphasis on reducing costs. ("The project would not become successful if we had gone on the cheap with the hotels," Cook later said.) Simply put, high quality was the way to go for future profitability. The gap between the two sides widened and entered a litigation phase.

Then things finally came to a head in June 2007 when the Cook Group's Blue Sky Corporation bought full control of the project and all litigation was dropped. There was a great sigh of relief in the Valley. The project had now come full circle with the Cook Group in control, and forging ahead. "We never fell off schedule," Bill Cook reported. Also, Cook, who had not been in on some of the early planning meetings, set a plan in place for having it redone to his satisfaction, and within a year, work began on the casino. As the grand opening approached, the finishing touches on both hotels brought out the elegance and beauty to a miraculous degree.

Conrad Schmitt Studios

The remarkable finishing work of the artisans from Conrad Schmitt Studios provided a final layer of elegance. This nationally renowned company had done work for the Cooks before, and had a long history which included excellent work in the decoration, restoration, and renovation of buildings exuding historical and architectural significance from the Waldorf Astoria in New York City to Union Station in St. Louis. Founded in 1889 in Milwaukee by Schmitt, the son of Bavarian immigrants, the company has over the last 75 years been run by three generations of the Gruenke family, providing gilding, glazing, marbleizing, stain glass design and conservation, decorative painting, faux finishes, plaster restoration, statuary sculpture and more. Their magical touch can be seen all around the grand hotels of Springs Valley. Now the excitement grew as the project moved toward completion.

THE HONORS BEGIN

While there is not a decisive moment when the job got 'finished,' a 2007 Gala was a crowning moment where Bill, Gayle and Carl Cook were the first to be honored with the 'Cook Cup for Outstanding Restoration.' In the crowd proudly watching was Representative Denbo, and at the podium speaking was the chairman of Historic Landmarks, Randall T. Shepard. Things had again come full circle: Denbo, Historic Landmarks, Cooks.

Randall Shepard, also the highly respected Chief Justice of the Indiana Supreme Court, and a trustee of the National Trust for Historic Preservation, gave a moving tribute to the Cooks. He made a point that the Cooks "had a vision of meticulously restored and thriving historic hotels, with a casino to visit, but not the only reason." And he predicted that someday the grand hotels of Springs Valley would become "tourist destinations to rival the Greenbrier Homestead."

Bill Cook was touched by the event, and the words from Shepard. Even after all the honors showered on him over the years, Cook remarked, "Nothing compares to that night."

The Public Comes

Those early visitors from the reopening up to 2010 couldn't believe their eyes. "It's almost too much to take in at once." "Everywhere you turn, there's something breathtaking." "Awesome." "Who made this happen?" were common comments. And althougoh America went into a 'great recession' just months later, the new/old resort in Springs Valley is attracting new and returning patrons who often say, "It's a miracle." And one can hope that when Bill Cook walks the grounds, he enjoys going over in his mind the enormity of what he has caused to transpire.

Meanwhile, although Bill Cook feels there are "still a hundred things left to do," he and Gayle, and their son Carl can stand as saviors of the magnificent grand hotels, and their amenities. Springs Valley in rural southern Indiana once again is one of the nation's great escapes!

Putting It All Together
"We Relied on Each Other" -Bill Cook

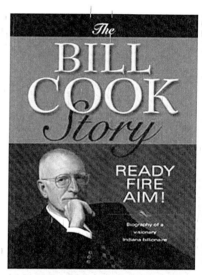

The extraordinary people that Bill Cook has surrounded himself with over the years and during the remake of the grand hotels, is a central theme in Hamell's remarkable biography. First, of course, Bill Cook's wife Gayle has been a driving force in renovation for years; and son Carl, a major part of the team, already a force in the huge job of eventually following in his father's footsteps.

Following are some of those who played central roles in the original, and the remaking of the grand hotels.

Steve Ferguson

Long time associate, Steve Ferguson, Cook's high profile right-hand man for many years, and the CEO of the Springs Valley project is central to all that Cook does. Ferguson was a 4-term state legislator, and more recently a central member of the Indiana University Board of Trustees.

Legendary Golf Architect
Donald Ross

Master Golf Designer Pete Dye

The 'Johnny Appleseed'
of American golf,
Thomas Bendelow

Bill Cook speaks very highly of his long time close associate, Steve Ferguson, who also is an avid golfer; who took the lead for Cook on re-doing the well-known *Donald Ross Hill Course* and the *Thomas Bendelow Valley Course*, and most recently the *Pete Dye Course*, which has the highest expectations of any new course in America. Bill Cook reports, "Steve has become very close to Pete Dye and Pete's idiosyncrasies ... he is a master golf designer."

Harrison Albright

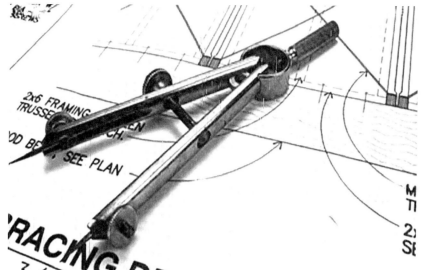

George Ridgeway

According to Cook, architect George Ridgeway is "the most renowned in the state. His reputation spreads all over the country." George Ridgeway, who is to Cook what Harrison Albright was to Sinclair a century ago, is one of those brilliant American architects who loves and studies the past, and re-imagines it for the world anew with the various challenges that Mr. Cook puts before him at any time. Brought up in a small town in Indiana, Ridgeway, over time, displayed brilliance in the simplicity of his work, a trait that is common among the best of architects. In conversation, Ridgeway explained to me how he was "correcting the design of the casino" by re-modeling it after the fabled Brown's Casino which in the first half of the 20th Century stood as a symbol of defiance and ur-elegance as French Lick's own little Las Vegas before there was a Las Vegas. Ridgeway's sense of history, humor, practicality, and artistry is evident in one architectural choice! Ridgeway spoke to an "opening day" festivities audience: "I've spent eleven years of my life waiting for this day, eleven years of being in this building, having a key to everything, able to go any time, any place, check out anything. Today I turn it over to the world. And my key doesn't go any place." Ridgeway feels there is another five or six years of work left on the project: "It's a 3,000-acre site with over 70 buildings. Building is still going on, but it's not full bore like it was."

Mr. Cook praises the Pritchetts for being, "efficient and proficient. What wonderful eyes they have for quality and detail," he adds of their long time association with the Cook Group.

The Visionaries

Denbo

Williamson

Cook

It is important to note that those who did the right things at the right time show a true respect for one another's efforts over the last two decades that is really touching: Denbo taking on the challenge of doing everything on Earth he could to get the state legislature behind him --which took thirteen years; Williamson with fighting to save an historic old building when it was falling down and seemed an impossible task; Cook incrementally saving, first the iconic old building from slow decay then saving the whole 'valley' from collapse, are all feats of superhuman determination over time. But all these years later, Denbo refers to Cook as an angel, and Williamson as a 'savior.' Williamson thinks of it as an extraordinary effort by those willing to stay the course, and Cook says to Denbo in a 2007 note, "We did it together."

Cook has made Historic Landmarks one of the major beneficiaries of funding from the hotel's profits. Denbo has retired to French Lick and spends time admiring the fruits of his efforts and business endeavors; Williamson has retired to Savannah GA, and has fond memories and great appreciation for the results that Cook brought to the effort. Cook, still going strong, is still doing finishing touches: "A hundred things to still do."

From the moment in the 1990s when Bill Cook decided to help Historic Landmarks save the West Baden Springs Hotel, literally from collapsing, the incredible journey of resurrection began. And slowly, through the following years, it became what Bill Cook described as "The largest preservation project ever attempted in this country, including Grand Central Station."

WHAT MAKES A HOTEL GRAND

Finally, what is a grand hotel, and what is it that so attracts us to them? On one level, we relax to be amidst the beauty that surrounds us in almost every direction. We are brought into the lovely world of pleasure, which elevates our sensibilities to the point of escaping daily drudgery, and, yes, time stops for a while. Much has been written over the years about 'pleasure,' and 'the pursuit of happiness.' Most people feel that pleasure is the sweetest of earthly accomplishments, and, of course, 'the pursuit of happiness' is as important as 'liberty,' and 'life' itself.

Pleasure has been defined as the fulfillment produced by enjoyment, or the expectation of good things happening to us. And happiness is the latter end of pleasure where there is satisfaction in the heart, the mind, and the soul.

It is no surprise that the ancient Greek philosopher, scholar and prolific writer, Epicurus should conclude that "pleasure is the beginning and end of living happily." Epicurus argued that the pleasures of the soul --especially contemplation-- is the greatest gift, and a school of philosophy extolling the seeking of pleasure and happiness, guided by morality, temperance, and serenity, now bears his name: Epicureanism.

In Springs Valley, for contemplation, you can take a short ride in a vintage Pullman's car for a few miles amidst some of nature's most natural beauty, then return to the little train depot --now a museum-- that in its heyday a century ago was the dropping-off point for hundreds of guests a day. You can imagine them from Chicago, and many other surrounding cities traveling to tiny French Lick Indiana to stay at one of the two grand hotels, or one of the many smaller hotels in town. Of those days when the trains ran to and from everywhere, and the elegance of the grand hotels was taken for granted. Well, much of that is back today, thanks mostly to a Southern Indiana family called Cook.

AFTERWARD
"Little Did We Know" -Gayle Cook

It seems to me that one of the best ways to put into perspective the meaning of the extraordinary remaking of Springs Valley's grand hotels, their amenities, and casino is to see it first through how Bill and Gayle Cook have done preservation in the past, and how their true altruism was the guiding philosophy behind the urge to do certain things simply because they need to be done.

In Bill and Gayle Cook's long partnership in extraordinary renovations over the years, they've been a real team: "Bill likes the bricks, the mortar ... I like the research, the history," explains Gayle Cook.

But their passion for preservation was a long time in the making. And it's a wonderful story, going back to when as a business the Cook company was chartered in 1963, a year after son Carl was born. The young family would take Sunday drives, for their "amusement." Gayle reports that Carl was "an easy, happy kid, even as a baby, we were always able to travel with him."

From the house in Bloomington, they would take rides around the Southern Indiana countryside, always on the lookout for interesting locations to check out, especially those with a connection to history. This led them to publish, in 1972, *A Guide to Southern Indiana*. Written by Gayle and Bill Cook, it emphasized the splendor of the rural life that Southern Indiana is one of the best examples of in America. In the introduction, Gayle, who is originally from Evansville, on the Ohio in the Southwest corner of Indiana, wrote of the "many surprises of the traveler who takes the side roads ... he should not be afraid to get lost. Some of out best discoveries were the results of unplanned meandering." The 'Guide' was very well received. *The Evansville Express* reported:

> "A lively browse through the Cook's booklet is quite enough to convince a person ... there is no need to drive to New England or the Grand Canyon merely to see the sights."

Over the years the company grew up along with Carl, and the family. And among the 'meanderings' the Cooks engaged in was a discovery that would be fateful years later. Gayle Cook tells of pictures of her parents standing outside the West Baden Springs Hotel: "I can't remember when we first saw it [but] I remember stopping by when the Jesuits were there. Then Bill and I saw it several times. Little did we know."

The Future

Carl Cook is a quiet, very intelligent 48 year-old man who can lucidly explain the balance of ingredients in the 1901 concrete used to build the original West Baden grand hotel, or speculate what the world might be like 400 years from now. Seated in his rounded tasteful office in the spacious Cook Group headquarters in Bloomington, Indiana in 2009, he is relaxed, contemplative, and totally forthcoming in answering questions about what the future of Springs Valley might look like and be like. "More attractions," he says, as he rubs his chin and turns his head toward the large window that looks out over the building's hotels- "a trolley that runs between the two hotels." (Taggart did the same from 1908-1919.) "More buildings around the hotels .... Upcoming at the Dye Golf Course, there'll be qualifiers for the PGA in 2010, and there's talk of more golfing events upcoming ... a 'dinner train' between French Lick and Jasper" (a sizeable affluent town 20 miles west of Springs Valley) ... and more.

He adds that he wants to see more convention buisness for the hotels. Then he adds with a warm smile, "a festival type convention for example, the national Model A [Ford] meeting will be held at West Baden this summer." To the question of how he prioritizes his various interests, he makes the point that the wide array of medical business he'll be taking over will be central, but, he wonders, "in 400 years who knows what diseases will even still exist? But those buildings [the hotels] will still be there."

Carl Cook is noticebly comfortable in his own skin, and is relaxed about taking over one day, but he also alludes to the importance of the contribution of the Cook Group's highly capable employees. He also points out that the re-opening of the hotels has brought well over 1000 new jobs (most for Orange County residents), and noticeably lowered the unemployment rate in the area.

In talking about the staples of mineral water and gambling that were behind the early success of the hotels, Carl Cook points out that there has been a resurgence of interest in spas recently and there is plenty of "the waters" springing forth from the Pluto Well at French Lick, and Sprudel at West Baden is also open. (The other wells are either capped off, or dormant.) He sees gambling as very important to the hotels' financial success.

There is no question that the younger Mr. Cook has a wide 'understanding' and firm grip on the future of the beautifully restored grand hotels. People from the area, and those who visit from far and wide, can cerainly rest easy that there will likely be a seamless transition from one generation of Cooks to another.

When asked of Carl how he feels things are going with the whole project, he responds that he is pleased about how the hotels are doing, and very confident of future profitability. When asked how he feels about being the proprietor of a great fortune, he answers in the tone of someone who's thoroughly thought it through: quite simply he regards money as "a tool" to do things. (The popular writer Cleveland Amory, a half century ago, wrote, "Midwesterners know how to make money, but they don't know how to spend it." He certainly mustn't have known Midwesterners like the Cooks.)

Finally, preservations. His whole face lights up, and to the question of whether he remembers those "meanderings" on Sundays with his parents around Southern Indiana: "I can remember back to when I was three." But he corrects me for referring to meanderings, "They [his parents] were '*looking for*' something," he says emphatically. And this suddenly makes a new kind of sense to me. Yes, it has to do with aesthetic sensibility but also with purpose. The Cooks *did* and *do* something about the things they lovingly look for, and then *find*. It seems that they want to preserve the inherent beauty of the past, so that they, and millions of others can find pleasure and happiness long into the future. When asked what is behind his urge to do preservation, he answers, because of "the fun."

There are not many stories that have happy endings these days. But this is one. You can tell it by the joy that exudes from the many hotel guests who travel to Springs Valley and enter a fantasy world that turns out to be so real that it astonishes. And if we end with a metaphor it is that the urge to preserve beauty is like the pursuit of happiness.

...THE END

Bill Cook

And Now...

Eighteen months after the refurbished hotels opened as French Lick Springs Resort Casino, there were clear signs that the future was going to be bright. Despite a difficult economy, an enthusiastic parade of vacationers, curious about the enormous re-making of the grand hotels in Springs Valley, came, saw, and were amazed.

The Springs Valley area received a great boost in jobs, economic development and pride, all at once, when the resort officially opened near the end of 2007, they employed "1,686 people in mostly newly created positions. Fifty-seven percent were filled by Orange county residents, causing the greatest drop in unemployment rate in the state." By 2009, employees from Orange County represented well over sixty percent of the workforce.

The coffers of the Towns of French Lick Springs and West Baden Springs each received $2 million per year through a "local development agreement" worked out in advance.

Orange County schools have received $100,000 per year also because of the "development agreement," and an extra $130,000 for Springs Valley Community Schools.

During 2007 alone, the Resort spent $17,500,000 on materials and services from Indiana Vendors.

The Indiana Department of Workforce Development announced that since the re-opening, 400 new jobs have been created in Orange County, (e.g. in retail, government positions, medical/legal) as a direct result of the resort's re-opening.

The 'local development' agreement also brought in $455,360 for Orange County communities beyond Springs Valley. Because of revenue created by the resort's casino admissions and wager taxes, the town of French Lick has been able to greatly improve community living conditions: repaired sidewalks and streets, beautification programs, new town vehicles (such as a 100-foot aerial ladder fire truck, police cars, and upgraded water plant trucks), and for the first time in eighty years, the town has been able to undertake a major downtown redevelopment program: a $15 million development project that includes dining, new retail facilities, residential housing, civic buildings, and "green" spaces.

Of the many charitable events initiated by the resort, a $250,000 boost for a fundraiser that helped the Indiana Historic Landmarks Foundation raise one million dollars.

In fiscal 2008, admission and wagering taxes from all Indiana gaming establishments came to $812,161,978.

New Activity

New developments in light of the 'grand re-opening' include a new hotel, 'Big Splash Mountain'(featuring a huge waterslide), a Comfort Inn -- and nearby movie theater, a new town center (Springs Stadium), a new West Baden Town Hall, new restaurants, a major pharmacy --the first in years-- and signs of new life with repaired homes, repaired streets and gardens now dotting the town.

Awards

2007: Bill and Gayle Cook receive the award for 'outstanding renovation' given by the Indiana Historic Landmarks Foundation.

November 2008: The renovated West Baden Springs Hotel was ranked in the top 100 (of 2000 resorts in America) rated by the prestigious travel magazine *Conde Nast Traveler*.

Also, it "is ranked in the first 25 of the Top 75 Mainland US Resorts. The national historic landmark is tied for 21st place with Enchantment Resort in Sedona and the Inn on Mount Ada on Catalina Island. With a score of 902, West Baden outranked well-known resorts such as the Wynn Las Vegas, The Greenbrier and the American Club when it was evaluated on activities/facilities, food/dining, location, overall design, rooms and services." What is most surprising is that West Baden Springs Hotel was abandoned as a hotel for most of the 20th Century, and less than two years after its remaking it received such a high rating.

January 2009: The West Baden Springs Hotel is placed on the very exclusive "Gold List" of the 710 best hotels, resorts, and cruise lines in the world.

Special Thanks

First, I'd like to thank the many local people I've had hundreds of conversations with about Springs Valley over the years. Their love of the history and lore ties into their own histories, and becomes part of the great American story. Their names are too numerous to mention, but I would advise visitors and guests to strike up conversations with them. It can be an unforgettable part of a visit.

Also, I would like to thank the management, staff, and employees of the hotels who have been gracious, helpful, and considerate. It is amazing how many who work, or have worked at the hotel, have shown me moments of the past that tie their personal history to the hotels. Also, I want to thank the many guests (from far and near) who have taken their time to chat and give their impressions. They have helped frame the tone of this book with stories from three or four generations. Over and over they have expressed their deep appreciation for the remaking of the hotels. And their excitement over Springs Valley as a place to visit has returned.

Appreciation for pictorial and graphic work from Pam Summerville at the Cook Group, and computer consultant Michael Bosworth.

I would also like to congratulate the many business leaders, Indiana politicians, Democratic and Republican, who were instrumental in making the long legislative process for gaming, spearheaded by Representative Denbo, Bob Alderman, Pat Bauer, Larry Conrad, Doyle Cornwell, Robert Denbo, Charles Hall, Lindel Hume, John Keeler, Mark Lytle, Paul Mannweiler, Jim Mathers, Bob Meeks, Mike Phillips, and the key Valley residents who spent many years of supporting the process, especially Everett Land, Claude Taylor, Jack Carnes, Grant Marshall, school administrators throughout Orange County, Imojean Detrick of the Orange County Foundation, friends Bill Reynolds, Max Apple, and many more.

Those who also made a huge difference: the staff of the Cook Group, the staff of the Historic Landmarks Foundation over the years – and the entire community of Springs Valley. Two people of special note: historian Jeff Lane and photo collector Dr. Clay Stuckey. I would especially like to thank Mary Lou Szczesiul for her photo design, Marilyn Longmire for her drawings, and Brad McNulty and Amanda McNeal for their contemporary photos.

And last, I'd like to thank my own family, half of which has a history in Southern Indiana stretching back to the 19th Century. They have also helped make the making of this book a pleasure.

In future editions, we'd like to call attention to others not included in this edition who have also helped keep the dream alive. You are invited to write to:

CMcN Books 1000 Waterway Boulevard, Indianapolis, Indiana 46202

BIBLIOGRAPHY

General References

Ballard, Charles Edward "Ed" with Janet Kirk Johnson and Anna Marie Borcia. *The Ballards in Indiana: A Story of Determination, Self-Education and Ultimate Success.* Indianapolis: C.E. Ballard-Literary Trust, 1984.

Blatchley, W.S., *The Mineral Waters of Indiana, Indianapolis*, Indiana 1903.

Bowers, Claude G. *Beverage and the Progressive Era.* Cambridge, Massachusetts: Houghton Mifflin, 1932.

Bundy, Chris. *West Baden Springs Legacy of Dreams.* Self published.

Carlson, Oliver, and Ernest Sutherland Bates. *Hearst: Lord of San Simeon.* New York: The Viking Press, 1936

Cottman, George S. *Centennial History and Handbook of Indiana.* Indianapolis: Max R. Hyman, Publishers, 1915.

Dillard, Arthur L. *Orange County Heritage.* Paoli, Indiana: Stout's Print Shop, 1971.

_____. *Power and Responsibility: The Life and Times of Theodore Roosevelt.* New York: Farrar, Straus and Cudahy, 1961.

Dunn, Jacob Platt, *Indiana and Indianans*, Vol I-V. Chicago and New York, 1919-1924.

Hammel, Bob, *The Bill Cook Story,* Indianapolis: Indiana University Press, 2009.

Kettleborough, Charles, *Constitution Making in Indiana, Indiana Historical Collection*, I (3vols, Indianapolis, Indiana 1916-1930).

Hofstader, Richard. *The Age of Reform: From Bryan to F.D.R.* New York: Alfred A. Knopf, 1955.

Hubbard, Kin, ed. *A Book of Indiana.* The Indiana Biographical Association, 1929.

Jensen, Richard J. *The Winning of the Midwest: Social and Political Conflict*, 1888-1896. Chicago: University of Chicago Press, 1971.

_____. *The President Makers: The Culture of Politics and Leadership in an Age of Enlightenment, 1896-1919.* New York: Harcourt, Brace and Company, 1938.

Lindley, Harlow, ed. *Indiana As Seen by Early Travelers,* Indianapolis, 1916.

Link, Arthur S. *The Higher Realism of Woodrow Wilson and Other Essays.* Nashville: Vanderbilt University Press, 1971.

McCarty, C. Walter, ed. *Indiana Today.* New Orleans: The James O. Jones Company, 1942.

McCombs, William F. *Making Woodrow Wilson President.* New York: Fairview Publishing Company, 1921.

Marshall, Thomas R. *Recollections of Thomas R. Marshall, Vice-President and Hoosier Philosopher: A Hoosier Salad.* Indianapolis: The Bobbs-Merrill Company, 1925.

Mowry, George E. *The Era of Theodore Roosevelt, 1900-1912.* New York: Harper, 1958

Older, Mrs. Fremont. *William Randolph Hearst: American.* New York: D. Appleton-Century Company, 1936.

Phillips, Clifton J. *Indiana in Transition: The Emergence of an Industrial Commonwealth, 1880-1920*. Indianapolis Historical Bureau and Indiana Historical Society, 1968.

Schlesinger, Arthur M., Jr., ed. *History of American Presidential Elections, 1789-1968*. Vol. 5. New York: Chelsea House Publishers, 1985.

Smith, Alfred E. *Up to Now: An Autobiography.* New York: The Viking Press, 1929.

Stoll, John B. *History of Indiana Democracy,* 1816-1916. Indianapolis: Indiana Democratic Publishing Company, 1917.

Swanberg, W.A. *Citizen Hearst: A Biography of William Randolph Hearst.* New York: Charles Scribner's Sons, 1961.

Trissal, Francis M. *Public Men of Indiana: A Political History*, 2 vols. Hammond, Indiana: W.B. Conkey Company, 1923.

Year Book of the State of Indiana for the Year 1917, Indianapolis: Wm. B. Burford, 1918.

Articles

Blackburn, Glen A. "Interurban Railroads of Indiana." *Indiana Magazine of History* (20 September 1924).

"Brethren of the Senate: Senator Taggart," *The Indiana Freemason* 48, no 4. (September 1970).

Clark, Martin and Wayne Curtis, "George Ridgeway's One Fine Architect," *Indiana State University Magazine* 2009.

"Denbo Retires from State House," *Associated Press*, 8 November 2007.

Frosch, Dr. William A., Dept of Psychiatry. "Taking the Waters –Springs, Wells, Spas," *The FASEB Weill Cornell Medical College* July 2007

Garrett, "French Lick Returns to Its Sin City Roots," *New York Times*, 16 March 2007.

Harper's Weekly, (13 August and 24 September 1904).

Hill, Herbert R. "Lost River Valley Meccas: West Baden and French Lick, A Classic Springs Rivalry." *Outdoor Indiana* 61 (November 1976).

"Casino Gambling Stirs Land Boom, *Indianapolis Star* 6 February 2006.

Jewell, Mark, "French Lick Casino Could Become Reality, *Associated Press*, 6 August 2003.

Moster, Mary Beth. "Whatever Happened to Pluto Water?" *Indianapolis Star Magazine*, 27 July 1975

Nicholson, Meredith, "T.T." *The Shield* (January-February 1928).

O'Malley, John W., S.J., "The Story of The West Baden Springs Hotel." *Indiana Magazine of History* 54 (December 1958

Painter, Carl: "The Progressive Party in Indiana." *Indiana Magazine of History* 16 (September 1920).

Rogers, Joseph C., "Letter Giving Analysis of Mineral Waters of French Lick," *Western Journal of Medicine* (December, 1869).

Rubino, Michael, "Town Hopes Casino Brings Gilded Age," *New York Times* 26 October 2006.

Silverman, Francine, "Elegance Returning to Midwest's Largest Resort," *Hotel Online*, October 1997.

Simons, Richard S. "When Grandpa and Grandma Took the Waters." *Indianapolis Star Magazine*, 9 August 1959.

Wright, Ruth, "Orange County's Casino Gamble," *The Round About*, November, 2003.

Pamphlets, Papers, and Miscellaneous Sources

"America Takes the Water Cure," *Readers' Digest* XXIX (October, 1936).

Associated Press, "Gambling Debate Never Ends," 12 February 2008.

Conrad Schmitt Studios Newsletter (30 December 2008).

Drake, Lisa, Paper on Mt. Arie, circa 1986, Melton Public Library, French Lick Indiana

French Lick Sesquicentennial History, "Ed Ballard," July 2008.

French Lick Sesquicentennial History, "Pluto Water," 5 September 2008.

Haupt, Richard Walter, "History of French Lick Springs Hotel." Master's Thesis, Indiana University, 1953.

Hotel Online, 11 April 2005.

Las Vegas Sun, 5 November 2003.

Lerollyn, John S., M.D. *The Rise and Fall of Mineral Springs Health Resorts in Southern Indiana*, Published Speech given at Pendermis Club, Louisville, KY, (10 February 1970).

"Pick-A-Package," brochure for French Lick Springs Golf and Tennis Resort (Paoli, Indiana 1985).

"Roll Call Indiana." *The Gaming Lawyer Forum*, 3 August 2005.

Sarbeck, Craig, *"The Springs at French Lick,"* Pamphlet History, 1979.

Springs Valley Herald, 22 July 1915

Stampp, *"Indiana Politics During The Civil War,"* (Indianapolis, 1949).

Structure Magazine, September 2007

"Thomas Taggart", *Who Was Who in America, I* (Chicago, 1942).

Index

Italicized page numbers refer to illusrations and photos

Abbott & Costello, 81, 106
Absolute Real Estate Auction, 118
Ade, George,
Aircrane, 128
Al Brown & Associates, 58
Al C. Barnes Circus, 98
Albright, Harrison, 41, 72, *139*
Alexander, "Silver Bob," 103
Algonquin, 10
Alma MI, 109
American Cabaret Company, 113, 124
Ames Cemetery, 104
Andrews, James M., 27
American Circus Corporation, 79, 98, 99
Amory, Cleveland, 145
Apollo, 20, 75, 118,
Architecture, 41
Arkansas Club, 60, 80
Arlington Hotel, 55
Army Hospital #35, see *US Army General Hospital #35*
Asclepius, 21
Athenaeum, 124
Atrium, 71-73, 75, 76, 81
Auction of French Lick Springs Hotel, 118
Austrians, 75
Automobile, 28, 51
Avenue Hotel, 55

Babylon Club, 56, 120
Baden, 21
Baden Baden, 36

Ballard, Chad, 63, 80, 103
Ballaard, Charles "Ed", 47, 60, 63, 65-70, 77-80, *81,* 98-100, 103, *104*
Ballard, Dolly, 63, 103
The Ballards in Indiana, 63, 103
Bally's French Lick, Inc., 134
Barnum, P.T., 37, 65, 70
Baseball, 62
Baths, 85 also see Pluto Water
Bauer, Speaker Pat, *132*
Beatty, Clyde, 98
Bedford Springs, 102
Beechwood, *63*
Bendelow, Thomas, *138*
Berlin, 114
Berlin, Irving, 63, 81, 95
Bicycle track, *35,* 71
Bird, Larry, 113, *134*
Bison, see *buffalo*
Black Sea, 63
Bloomington, 142, 142
Blue Sky, 134-135
Boone, Daniel, 8
Bowers, Bert, 98
Bowles, Eliza, 26
Bowles, Julia, 27
Bowles Spring, *48,* 94
Bowles, Thomas C., 14
Bowles, Dr. William A, 14, *15, 16,* 17-20, 23, 25-27
Bowling alley, 74
Boyd, Julia, 95

Boykin Group, 123, 129
Brady, Nicholas, F., 95
Brecht, Bertolt, 114
Bredit, Eliza, 33,
Brown, Al, 58
Brown's Casino, *46,* 47, 56, 80. 86, *106,* 107, 139
Bruin, Frank, 99
Bryant, William Jennings, 54
Buffalo traces, 6, 9, 12, 14
Bunyan, John, 52
Buskirk, Judge, 50
Burton Hote, *55*
Byzantines, 41

Cabaret, 114
Cabot, John B., 106
Caldwell and Drake, 41
California, 17, 115
Calliope, 75, 140
Cape Cod, *90*
Caiptol Avenue, 88
Capone, Al, *97*
Carnegie
Carned, Jack, 130
Carlsbad, 36
Carlsbad of America, *43, 87*
Casinos, *46,* 47, 56 see *gambling*
Casino Nationalle, 99
Cedar Farms, 125
Celtics, 113
Charles, William, 11
Charleston, W.VA., 72

151

Chicago, 33, 78, 80, 81, 87, 97, 109, 111, 114, 141
Chicago Cubs, 62
Chicago Daily Tribune, 40
Chicago Mob, 59
Chinese, 116
Chicago Railroad, 29
Christian Bible, 21
Cincinnati, 111, 114
Cincinnati Reds., 62
Circassia, 63
Circus, 64-70, 100, *see Hagenbeck-Wallace Circus, and American Circus Corporation*
Civil War, 25, 33
City Hotel, 55
Clark, George Rogers, 8, 9
Claude McNeal Productions, 114
Claxton Hotel, 55
Clio, 75, 140
Cloverdale, 33
Club Chateau, 120
Colonial Club, 56
Colonial Hotel, 55
Common Prayer, Book of, 92
Congress Hotel, 78
Congreve Hotel, 80
Conrad, Larry, 121
Conrad Schmitt Studio, 135
Convention Hall, 82, 96, 113
Cook, Bill, 125, 126-128, 130-*133, 136, 137, 138, 139, 140,* 141, 142,
Cook, Carl, 136-138, 142-144
Cook Cup for Historic Preservation, 136
Cook, Gayle, 119, 125, 127, 130, 133, 136-139, 142, 143

Cook Group, 134, 135, 138, 139, 143
Coolidge, President Calvin, 89
Cooper, Lt. Harold, 77, 80
Corbett, James J., 62
Corinis, 20
Corinth, 21
Cory, CE, 65
Cos, 21
Cotrell, Mrs. 77
Cowboys, 8, 10
Cox Organization, 110-111
Crash, *see Stock Market Crash*
Crime, *see organized crime*
Crocker, Roger, 62
Crosby, Bing, 106
Crown Hill Cemebery, Salem IN, 71
Cuba, 80, 99

D-Day, 120
Dairy barn, 53
Dallas, 107
David, Governor Jefferson, 60
Dead Rat Club, 56, 120
Dean, Dizzy, 62
Democratic National Chairman, 49, 54, 60
Democratic National Party, 50, *54,* 88, 90, 93, 97, 120, 126, 130
Denbo, Representative Jerry, 119, *120,* 122, 124-131, *132,* 133, 136, *140*
Derby Weekend Raid, 106
Dickens, LT, 39
Dillingham, Charles B., 95
Dome, *41,* 62, 71-73, *75*
Domed Swimming Pool, 82
Donald Ross Golf Course, 135, 138
Donnelly, Father, 104

Dorsey Brothers, *112*
Dowden, Dr. CW, 80
Dudley, Frank A., 95
Durbin, Governor Winfield T., 42
Dutch, 9
Dye, Peter, *138*

Edison, Thomas, A., 28, 34, 139
Egypt, 41, 57
Eighth Wonder of the World, 42, 71, 76, 81 101, 126
Eisenhower, President Dwight, 108
Electric light, 28
Elite Cafe, 56, 120
Ellis House, 55
England, 15
English, 8
Entertainment at the hotels, 62, 71, *112-113*
Epicures, 141
Epidaurus, 21
Erickson Crane Company, 128
Errol, Leon, 95
Erwin Hotel, 55
Europe, 103, 105
Evans, Max, 128
The Evansville Express, 142

Fadely, James, 60
Famous Hill Golf Course, 135
Fairbanks, Senator Charles W, 42
Fairbanks, Crawford, 39
Ferber, Edna, 82
Ferguson, Steve, 134, *137*
Fire, 40, 48, *71-75*
Floor plan of dome, *41*
Florida, 103

Flu, 75, 76
Ford, Henry, 139
Forest Park IL, 79
Fort at French Lick, 10, 11, 13, 14
France, 10, 63
Francis, Rev. Joseph M, 92
Frederick County, Maryland, 15
Fredericks, Pauline, 95
French, 8, 9,
French and Indian War, 8
French Lick/ French Lick Springs, 7-13, 26, 28, 29, 65-70, 104, 105, 107, 113, 114, 116, 117, 118, 120, 124-126, 129, 132, 134, 135, 140-143
French Lick Casino, 130, 139, see gambling
French Lick Company, 83
French Lick Creek, 24
French Lick Gaming Bill, 132
French Lick House, 18
French Lick Sheraton, 110
French Lick Springs Golf & Tennis Resort, 110
French Lick Springs Hotel, 9, 15, 18, 20, 26, 29, 30, 32, 34, 35, 36, 48, 54-57, 62, 82, 83, 84, 85, 88, 93, 95, 96, 97, 102, 106, 107. 109-110, 112-114, 116-118, 121-123, 125, 126, 129, 134, 135
French Lick Springs Hotel Company, 39, 40
French Lick Springs Resort, 120, 139, 140
French Lick Springs Villas, Inc., 111, 113
Frest, R.E., 95

GI Bill, 108
Gagnon, George S, 49
Gala 2007, 136
Gambling, 47, 50, 56, 57, 58, 59, 60, 80, 106, 117, 120, 122, 130, 131-135
Games, 50
Gaming, *see gambling*
Garland, Judy, 106
Gates, John, W., 95
Gay 90s, 84
Germany 8, 75, 77

Golf, 53, 62, 63, 135, 139
The Gorge, 56
Graham-Paige Automobile Company, 100
Graham, Robert 100
Grand Casino, In. 125
Grand Central Station, 141
Grand Hotel, *55,* 88
Great Depression, 81, 93, 105, 106
Great Flu Epidemic, *see flu*
Great Train Crash, *78-79*
Greece, 21, 63
Green Country, 121
Green Acres Casino, 56
Greencastle, 33
Greeks, 57, 118, 141
Greek gods, 20
Greeley, Horace *17*
Gregg, Speaker John, 129
Grigsby Hous, 55
Gruenke, 135
A Guide to Southern Indiana, 142

Hagen, Walter, 63
Hagenbeck, Karl, 65
Hagenbeck-Wallace Circus, *64-68, 68*-70, 77, *78, 98*
Hammel, Bob, 125, 127, 131, 137
Hammond, IN, 78
Hanley, Indiana Governor, 50
Haupt, Richard, 95
Havana, 80, 99
Hearst, William Randolph, 50, *60*
Henderson, Ernest, 110
Hesiod, 21
Historic Landmarks Foundation, 119, *124,* 126, 128, 133, 136, 140
Historical Society of West Baden, 124
Homestead Hotel, 55
Hope, Bob, 106
Hoosier Club, 80
Hoover, Herbert, 89

Hospital, 711
Hot Springs, 80, 102
Hotel Clifton, 30, *31*
Hotel Pavillion, 30, *31,* 55
Hotel Windsor, *30,* 36, 48, 55
House Bill 1092, 132, 133
The Howard, 55
Howard, John C, 49
Howard, John L., 49
Hoyt, Robert, 133
Hygeia, 118

India, 57
Indians, 7, 8, 10, *11,* 12
Indiana Club, 56, 120
Indiana Gaming Commission, 129, *134, 135*
Indiana Statehood, 12-13
Indiana Statehouse, 129
Indiana Supreme Court, 26
Indiana Terriroty, 6, 8, 10, 12, 17
Indianapolis, 39, 88, 111, 114
Indianapolis Star, 103
Influenza, *see flu*
Inventions, *28*
Ireland, 38
Iroquois, 9, 10

Jacob's Entertainment, 134
James, Luther, *123*
James (Col. William) House, 125
Jazz Age, 112
Jefferson, Thomas 52
Jesuits, 10, 100, 101, 104, 109
John Robinson's Circus, 98
Johnson, Andrew, 25
Johnson, Harvey, 68

Kelley, Emmett, 98
Kennedy, John F., 38, 91
Kennedy, Joseph P., *90-91*

Kenny, William F, 95

Kentucky Club, 56, 80, 120
Kentucky Derby, 107, 120
Kern, John W, 54
Knights of the Golden Circle, 25
Kritchfield Company, 37

Lake Michigan, 125, 129
Land, Everett, 121
Lane, Dr. John A, 19, 20, 23. 24, 27
Las Vegas, 58, 106, 106, 117, 139
Lauth Group/Lauth Resorts & Casino, LLC, 134
Lawrence County, 121
Life Magazine, 128
Lilly, Eli, family, 124
Lincoln, Abraham, 25, 125
Lind, Jenny, 37
Lindley Inn, 55
Lottery, 120, see gambling
Louis XIV, 10
Louisiana Purchase, 17
Louisville, 6, 71, 103, 111, 114
Louisville Railroad, 29

MacAdamization/MacAdam, John London, 23
Madison Square Garden, 99, 103
Maloney, Frank, 116
Mannweiler, Paul, 126
Manyhan, County, 38
Marlin Properties, 115
Marshall, Governor Thomas, 54, 58
Marx Brothers, 100
Mathers, Jim, 130,
Mayans, 21
McDonald, Eugene, 115
McGuire, WA, 95
Mesopotamia, 41

Mexican War, 19
Miami, 80, 107
Miami Indians, 10, 65
Mile Lick, 20
Mineral Water, 22, 62, 102, *see Pluto Water*
Minnesota Investment partners, 125
Mississippian culture, 7
Mississippi, 19
Mob, *see organized crime*
Monon Railway, 29, 39, 53, 84, *96*, 107
Monte Carlo, 59
Moore, Robert, 100
Moorish towers, 42, 72
Mound builders, 7
Mount Airie, *90*, 91
Muckrakers, 52
Mulligan, Joh, 98
Murphy, Charles, F., 95
Murrow, Edward R., 108

National Democratic Party *see Democratic National Party*
National Tru;st for historic Preservation, 127, *136*
Nationalle, 80
New Albany Railroad, 29
New Haven, CT., 103
New York, 97, 103, 106, 113, 114, 135
New York Stock Exchange, 110 *see stock market*
New York Times, 93
New York World, 60
Nomadic tribes, 10, 12
Northwest Ordinance, 12
Northwood Institute, 109

Ohio River, 6, 12, 14, 18, 125, 129
O'Malley, John W., 37, 40, 42, 101
Opera House, *35*, 62, 71, 74, 112
Orange County, 15, 80, 95, 104, 114, 116, 117, 121-123, *130*-133, 143

Kentucky, 25, 103
Orange County Commission Against Legalized Gambling, 133
Orange County Courthouse, 50
Orange County Circuit Court, 26
Orange County Development, LLC, 134
Orange Shirts, 120, 130, 132
Ordinance of 1787, 9
Oregon Territory, 17
Organized Crime, *59*
Orleans, 130
Outstanding Hoosier Preservation Award, 131
Oxford Hotel, 56,
Oxford, Inn, 55

PGA, 63, 138, 143
Pacific War,
Pagodas, 75
Palm Island Club 80, 103
Pantheon, 41
Paoli, 15, 16, 50
The Paoli Republican, 33
Paris France, 114
Parker, Judge Alton, B., 54
Patoka Lake, 125, 126, 129
Perrin House, 55
Pershing, John J., 75
Persian Gulf, 118
Peru, IN, 65
Pete Dye Golf Course, 135, 138-139, 144
Phillips, Mike 122
Phonograph, 28
Philadelphia Phillies, 62
Pickford, Mary, *100*
Pilgrims Progress, 52
Pittsburgh Pirates, 62
Plant, MF, 95

Pluto devil, *50, 61,83, 94, 96*
Pluto Processing Plant, 61, 83, 106
Pluto Spring/ Pluto Water/Pluto Well, 26, *30, 31,* 36,*48,* 49, 50, 52, 61, 82, 83, 85, *88, 94,* 106, *107,* 143
Polk, James K, 19
Pompeian Court, 42, 80
Pratt, CL, 50
Printing Office at West Baden Springs Hotel, 53
Pritchett, Joe, 127, 128, *139*
Prohibition, 80
Promontory, Utah, 29
Proserpine Spring, 30, 48, 94
Pure Food and Drug Act, 52

Radio, 28
Railroad/Railway, 29
Reader's Digest, 102
Republican Party, 121, 122, 126, 130
Reconstruction, 26
Refrigeration, 28
Reinhart, Mary Roberts, 95
Renaissance, 41, 56
Rexford, Charles, 71, 74, 75, 80
Rhodes, AJ, 18
Ridgeway, George, 126, 127, 138, *139,* 143
Riley Estate, 103
Ringling, John, 99
Ringling Brothers Barnum & Bailey Circus, 99
Ritter House, 55, 56
Roaring 20s, 84
Rogers, Dr. DJ, 26
Rome, 21, 41, *57,* 101
Roosevelt, Franklin D, 97, 102
Roosevelt, Theodore, *52,* 54
Ross, Donald, 63, 135, *138*
Ross Golf Course, 138
Rotary Club, *81*

Round Tree Inn, 56
Round Trip Inn, 80
Rupert, Jake, 95
Ryan, George, 103
Ryan, Dr. Samuel, 26, 34
Ryan House, 55

Salem, 33
Salt Lick, 9
Salt Manufacturing, *13,* 14
Salt springs, wells, 5, 15, 17, 20, 21
Saratoga Springs, 55, 80, 102
Savannah, GA, 140
Schriker, Governor Henry F., 106, 120
Schweyer, 77
Sells-Floto Circus, *98*
Sharkey, William, 62
Shepard, Randall, T., 136
Sheraton, 110, 113, 123
Show Boat, 82
Showman's League of america, 79
Sinatra, Frank, 106
Sinclair, Lee Wiley, *33,* 35, 39, 40, 41, 43, 47, 48, 0, 51, 55, 58, 59, 63, 71, 72, 74, 76, 80, 112, 117
Sinclair, Lillian, 71, 72, 74, 75-77, 80
Sinclair, Thomas Taggart, 91
Skelton, Red, 98
Smith, Governor Al, 80,88,89,95
Society of Jesus, *see Jesuits*
Sousa, John Phillip, 112
Sparks Circus, *98*
Springs Valley, 7, 16, 22, 23,28, 50, 51, 52 55, 57, 58,60, 62, 65-70, 8 0, 83, 84, 95, 104-105, 107, 110, 113-116, 117,120, 123, 129, 132-138,143
Springs Valley Herald, 65-70

Springfield, MA, 110
Sprudel, *50,* 143
St. Louis, 10, 111, 114, 135
St. Louis Browns, 62
St. Louis Cardinals, 62
St. Paul's in London, 41
St. Peter's in Rome, 40, 41
Stouffer, Gary. 109
Stock Market Crash, 81, 99
Stonehaven Hotel, 110
Stowe, Harriet Beecher, 37
Streetcar, 51, *93*
A Streetcar Named Desire, 108
Sulfer, 22
Sullivan, Ed, 108
Sullivan, Johon L., 62
Sullivan, Roger, 95
Sutton Hotel, *55,* 56
Swift, Mayor, 62
Switzerland, 21

Taft, William Howard, 54
Taggart, Lucy, 85, *89*
Taggart, Thomas, Sr., 37, *38*-40, 47-63, 80, 82, 85, 88-97, *102,* 110, 143
Taggart, Thomas, Jr., 91, 97, *102,* 107
Tammany Hall, 62
Tea House Plantation, 62
Tennis, 62
Thalia, 75, 140
Thomas Bendelow Course, 138
Thomas Taggart, Biography by James Fadely, 60
Thomas Taggart Memorial, *92*
Thompson, Mayor "Big Bill.," 62, 81
Three Penny Opera, 114
Time Sharing, 111

Titanic, 118
Toliver Hotel, 55
Tomato juice, 86, *94*
Train Crash, *see Great Train Crash*
Tranchant Indiana LLC, 134
Transcontinental Railway, 29
Trappers, 7
Trump, Donald, *134*
Trump Indiana Casino Management, 134
Tunney, Gene, 95
Turner, Arthur, 109
Turner, Lana, 81, 95

Under the Dome, 75
Uncle Tom's Cabin, 37
Union Station, 84, 135
US Army General Hospital #35, *76*, 77
US Tent & Awning Company, 78
Utah, 29

Valley of the Salt Springs, *see Springs Valley*
Valley of the Salt Wells, 17
Vatican, 100
Vaudeville, 36-37
Villas, 111, 112
Vincennes, 6, 8, 12, 13, 14
Vogue Minstrel Troupe, 74
Vonnegut, Bernard, 124
Vonnegut, Kurt, 124

Wabash, 6, 8, 12, 18, 65
Waldorf Astoria, 135
Wall Street, 100
Wall Street, 81
Wallace, Benjamin, 65 *see Hagenbeck-Wallace Circus*

War Bond Drive, 106
Waters, curative, 21, 50, 52, *see Pluto Water*
Washington County, 121
The Wells Hotel, 55
Wells, Hirem W., 27
West Baden/West Baden Springs, 20, 24, 28, 29, 36, 65-70, 103-105, 109, *115*, 116-119, 122, 124-126, 129, 132, 139, 140, 142, 143
West Baden Springs Hotel Opera House, *see Opera House*
West Baden Water Company, 50
White Sulpher Springs, 102
Whiteman, Paul, *112*
Williams, Tennessee, 108
Williamson, J. Reid, 119, 124-125,*140*
Wilson, Woodrow, 54, 89
Windsor Hotel, *see Hotel Windsor*
Wininger, Barry, 133
Woodlawn Cemetery, 79
World War I, 63, 75, 76, 80
World War II, 105, 108, 112

Yucatan Peninsula, 21

Lobby, French Lick Springs Hotel 2010

Atrium, West Baden Springs Hotel 2010

Photos: Brad McNulty
Amanda McNeal